GOLF RULES IN PICTURES

A PUBLICATION OF
The United States Golf Association

Compiled and Edited by Joseph C. Dey, Jr.
Illustrated by George Kraynak

Publishers · GROSSET & DUNLAP · New York
A FILMWAYS COMPANY

LIBRARY OF CONGRESS CATALOG CARD NUMBER: CD62-273
ISBN: 0-448-01360-6

PRINTED IN THE UNITED STATES OF AMERICA

CONTENTS

INTRODUCTION

The Rules of Golf were first codified little more than 200 years ago by one organization — the Honourable Company of Edinburgh Golfers, in Edinburgh, Scotland. That initial code, written in 1744, consisted of 13 regulations, beginning with the instruction that "the ball must be teed within two club-lengths of the hole." How was the ball teed? On a little mound of soil. And where did the soil come from? Inside the hole, of course. When play of the hole was completed, the player merely scooped a little dirt from inside the hole, built a small mound and then set his ball upon it. So much for uniform-sized holes. The regulation that set the diameter of the hole at 4-1/4 inches and its depth at least 4 inches came much later.

The fact that the ball was teed within two club-lengths of the hole also meant that putting greens of two centuries ago were less than the impeccably groomed surfaces we see in our United States Open Championship of today. As conditions became more favorable for putting, inventive souls created new instruments to help them. One, for instance, attached a spirit level to his putter, but that was in violation of a Rule that had been developed much later than those original 13 regulations and designed to maintain the game in its traditional form.

Today the Rules are written by two organizations — the United States Golf Association and the Royal and Ancient Golf Club of St. Andrews, Scotland. These Rules are in effect wherever golf is played, whether it be a weekend four-ball at your Club or for many thousands of dollars on the professional tour. Representatives from both the USGA and the R & A meet regularly every four years to confer on the Rules and to make adjustments and to clarify them where it is deemed necessary, for golf is a dynamic game and the Rules must stay apace of new developments. Golf is played, also, over a vast expanse — indeed at least 125 acres is needed for a standard 18-hole course — and the opportunity for original and unusual situations is limitless.

The object of this book is to make some of the fundamental Rules situations come to life. The bare bones of the code are presented in drawings.

As you read *Golf Rules in Pictures,* note that the Rules present many rights for the player. It is not a code of purely restrictive covenants; rather it is an expression of all the golfing customs which generations of sportsmen have found fairest for all. The Rules are just a reflection of the sporting way of playing the game. They therefore carry privileges, as well as obligations.

In examining any picture and the relative text, the reader will find it worthwhile to refer to the complete Rule on the subject at the back of the book.

The illustrative material in this book was compiled by Joseph C. Dey, Jr., the former Executive Director of the United States Golf Association, C. Edmund Miller, Executive Assistant, and by myself.

P. J. BOATWRIGHT, JR.
Executive Director, United States Golf Association

ETIQUETTE

DON'T DELAY

Players should play without delay.

SAFETY FIRST

No player should play until the players in front are out of range.

SEARCHING FOR BALL—PLAYING THROUGH

Players searching for a ball should allow other players coming up to pass them; they should signal to the players following them to pass, and should not continue their play until those players have passed and are out of range.

CONSIDERATION FOR OTHER PLAYERS

No one should move, talk or stand close to or directly behind the ball or the hole when a player is addressing the ball or making a stroke.

ETIQUETTE

PRIORITY ON THE COURSE

If a match fails to keep its place on the course and loses more than one clear hole on the players in front, it should allow the match following to pass.

HOLES IN BUNKERS

Before leaving a bunker, a player should carefully fill up and smooth over all holes and footprints made by him.

RESTORE DIVOTS, REPAIR BALL-MARKS AND DAMAGE BY SPIKES

A player should make sure that any turf he has cut or displaced in fairway or rough is immediately replaced and pressed down.

On the putting green, a player should carefully repair damage made by his ball. After he and his companions have holed out, damage to the putting green caused by golf shoe spikes should be repaired.

DAMAGE TO GREENS

RIGHT

WRONG

Players should ensure that, when putting down bags, or the flagstick, no damage is done to the putting green, and that neither they nor their caddies damage the hole by standing close to it, in handling the flagstick or in removing the ball from the hole. The flagstick should be properly replaced in the hole before the players leave the putting green. Players should not damage the putting green by leaning on their putters, particularly when removing the ball from the hole.

DEFINITIONS

ADDRESSING THE BALL

A player has "addressed the ball" when he has taken his stance by placing his feet on the ground in position for and preparatory to making a stroke *and* has *also* grounded his club — except:

In a hazard he has addressed the ball when he has taken his stance preparatory to making a stroke. (He is not allowed to ground his club in a hazard.) **Definition 1.**

ADVICE

"Is my grip right?"

"Is the penalty one or two strokes?"

"Advice" is any counsel or suggestion which could influence a player in determining his play, the choice of a club, or the method of making a stroke. Information on the Rules or Local Rules is not advice. **Definition 2.**

BALL DEEMED TO MOVE

A ball has "moved" if it leave its position and come to rest in any other place. **Definition 3.**

[11]

DEFINITIONS

BALL LOST

"I've found your first ball!"

"I can't play that one — this one's in play now."

A ball is "lost" if:
  a. It be not found, or be not identified as his by the player, within five minutes after the player's side or his or their caddies have begun to search for it; or
  b. The player has put another ball into play under the Rules; or
  c. The player has played any stroke with a provisional ball from a point nearer the hole than the place where the original is likely to be. **Definition 6.**

"Here's your original ball."

"Too late. I've just played the provisional from here."

CASUAL WATER

"Casual water" is any temporary accumulation of water which is visible before or after the player takes his stance and is not in a water hazard. Snow and ice are either casual water or loose impediments, at the option of the player. **Definition 8.**

Not Casual Water

Casual water

[12]

GROUND UNDER REPAIR

"Ground under repair" is any portion of the course so marked by order of the Committee or so declared by its authorized representative. It includes material piled for removal and a hole made by a greenkeeper, even if not so marked. Stakes and lines defining ground under repair are in such ground. **Definition 13.**

HAZARDS; BUNKER

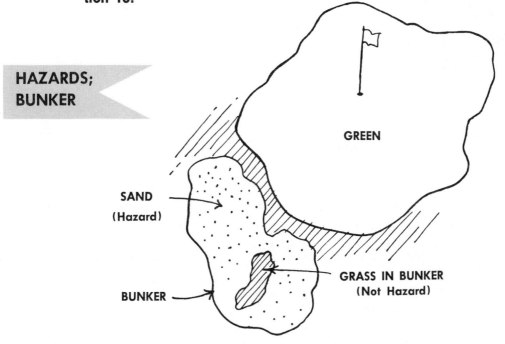

A "hazard" is any bunker, water hazard or lateral water hazard. It is the duty of the Committee in charge of a course to define accurately the extent of the water hazards. **Definition 14.**

A "bunker" is an area of bare ground, often a depression, which is usually covered with sand. Grass-covered ground bordering or within a bunker is *not* part of the hazard. **Definition 14a.**

DEFINITIONS

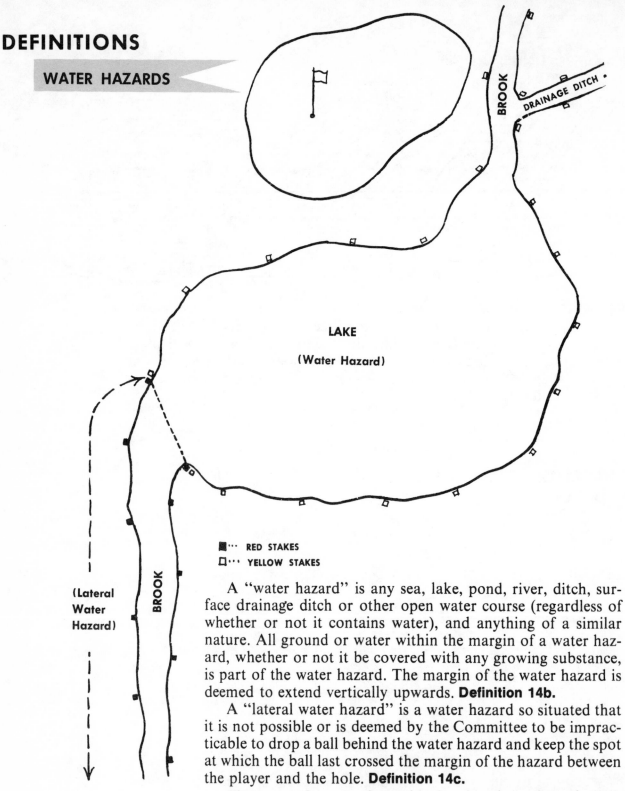

LAKE

(Water Hazard)

(Lateral Water Hazard)

BROOK

BROOK

DRAINAGE DITCH

■··· RED STAKES
□··· YELLOW STAKES

A "water hazard" is any sea, lake, pond, river, ditch, surface drainage ditch or other open water course (regardless of whether or not it contains water), and anything of a similar nature. All ground or water within the margin of a water hazard, whether or not it be covered with any growing substance, is part of the water hazard. The margin of the water hazard is deemed to extend vertically upwards. **Definition 14b.**

A "lateral water hazard" is a water hazard so situated that it is not possible or is deemed by the Committee to be impracticable to drop a ball behind the water hazard and keep the spot at which the ball last crossed the margin of the hazard between the player and the hole. **Definition 14c.**

That part of a water hazard to be played as a lateral water hazard should be distinctively marked. Stakes and lines defining the margins of hazards are in the hazards. **Definition 14**

Water hazards should be defined by yellow stakes or lines and lateral water hazards by red stakes or lines. **Definition 14 (Note).**

LOOSE IMPEDIMENTS

"Loose impediments" are natural objects not fixed or growing and not adhering to the ball, such as stones not solidly embedded, leaves, twigs, branches and the like, dung, worms and insects and casts or heaps made by them.

Snow and ice are either casual water or loose impediments, at the option of the player.

Sand and loose soil are loose impediments on the putting green, but not elsewhere on the course. **Definition 17.**

OBSTRUCTIONS

An "obstruction" is anything artificial, whether erected, placed or left on the course, including the artificial surfaces and sides of roads and paths but excepting:

   a. Objects defining out of bounds, such as walls, fences, stakes and railings;
   b. In water hazards, artificially surfaced banks or beds, including bridge supports when part of such a bank. Bridges and bridge supports which are not part of such a bank are obstructions;
   c. Any construction declared by the Committee to be an integral part of the course. **Definition 20.**

DEFINITIONS

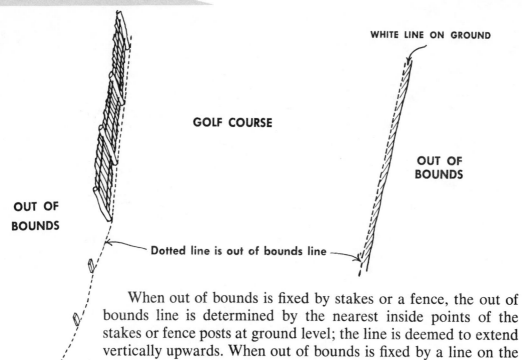

WHITE LINE ON GROUND

GOLF COURSE

OUT OF
BOUNDS

OUT OF
BOUNDS

— Dotted line is out of bounds line —

When out of bounds is fixed by stakes or a fence, the out of bounds line is determined by the nearest inside points of the stakes or fence posts at ground level; the line is deemed to extend vertically upwards. When out of bounds is fixed by a line on the ground, the line itself is out of bounds. A ball is out of bounds when all of it lies out of bounds. **Definition 21.**

OUTSIDE AGENCY—RUB OF THE GREEN

An "outside agency" is any agency not part of the match or, in stroke play, not part of a competitor's side, and includes a referee, a marker, an observer, or a forecaddie employed by the Committee. Neither wind nor water is an outside agency. **Definition 22.**

A "rub of the green" occurs when a ball in motion is accidentally stopped or deflected by any outside agency. **Definition 27.**

PARTS OF THE COURSE

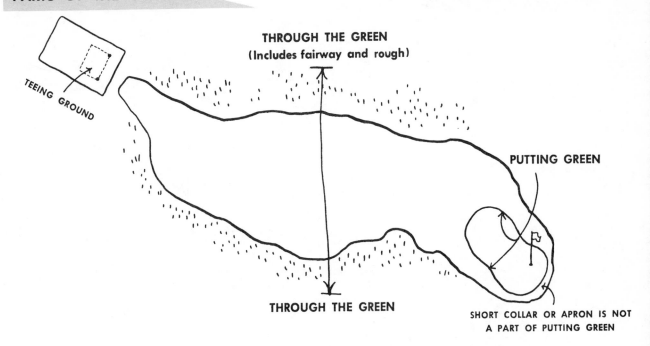

The "putting green" is all ground of the hole being played which is specially prepared for putting or otherwise defined as such by the Committee.

A ball is deemed to be on the putting green when any part of it touches the putting green. **Definition 25.**

The "teeing ground" is a rectangular area two club-lengths in depth, the front and the sides of which are defined by the outside limits of two tee-markers. A ball is outside the teeing ground when all of it lies outside the stipulated area. When playing the first stroke with any ball from the teeing ground, the tee-markers are immovable obstructions. **Definition 33.**

"Through the green" is the whole area of the course except:
a. Teeing ground and putting green of the hole being played;
b. All hazards on the course.

Definition 35.

DEFINITIONS

Definition 28

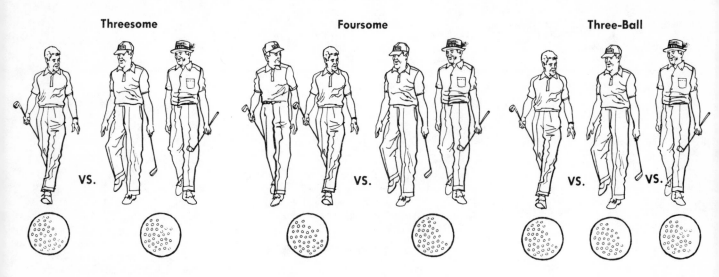

Threesome	Foursome	Three-Ball

A threesome is a match in which one plays against two, and each side plays one ball.

A foursome is a match in which two play against two, and each side plays one ball.

A three-ball is a match in which three play against one another, each playing his own ball.

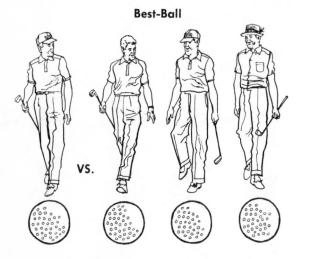

Best-Ball

A best-ball is a match in which one plays against the better ball of two or the best ball of three players.

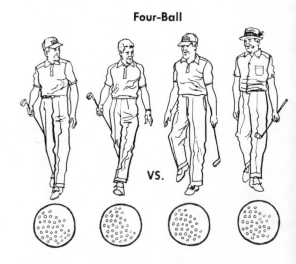

Four-Ball

A four-ball is a match in which two play their better ball against the better ball of two other players.

STROKE

A "stroke" is the forward movement of the club made with the intention of fairly striking at and moving the ball.

Definition 31.

THE RULES OF PLAY

**STIPULATED ROUND;
THE GAME**

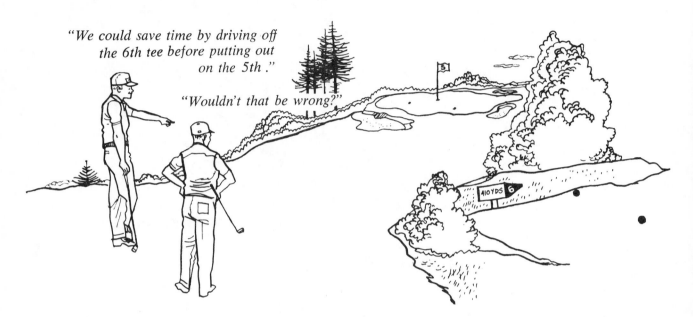

"We could save time by driving off the 6th tee before putting out on the 5th ."

"Wouldn't that be wrong?"

The "stipulated round" consists of playing the holes of the course in their correct sequence unless otherwise authorized by the Committee. The number of holes in a stipulated round is 18 unless a smaller number is authorized by the Committee.

In match play only, the Committee may, for the purpose of settling a tie, extend the stipulated round to as many holes as are required for a match to be won. **Definition 30.**

The Game of Golf consists in playing a ball from the teeing ground into the hole by successive strokes in accordance with the Rules. PENALTY: *Match play—Loss of hole; Stroke play—Disqualification.* **Rule 1.**

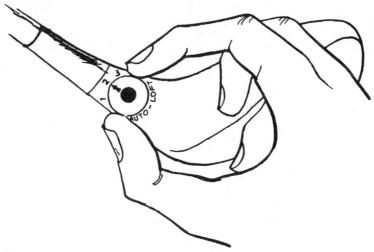

All of the parts of the club shall be fixed so that the club is one unit; the club shall not be designed to be adjustable, except for weight. Its playing characteristics shall not be purposely changed during a round; foreign material shall not be added to the club face at any time. PENALTY: *Disqualification.* **Rule 2-2a, 2b**.

THE GRIP

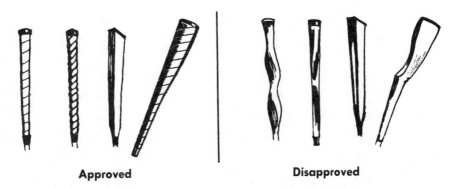

Approved   **Disapproved**

The grip consists of that part of the shaft designed to be held by the player and any material added to it for the purpose of obtaining a firm hold. The grip shall be substantially straight and plain in form, may have flat sides, but shall not have a channel or a furrow or be molded for any part of the hands. **Appendix IId.**

A device designed to give the player artificial aid in gripping the club is prohibited even though it be not part of the grip. (Exceptions: Plain gloves and material or substance applied to the grip, such as tape, gauze or resin.) PENALTY: *Disqualification.* **Rule 37-9.**

THE BALL

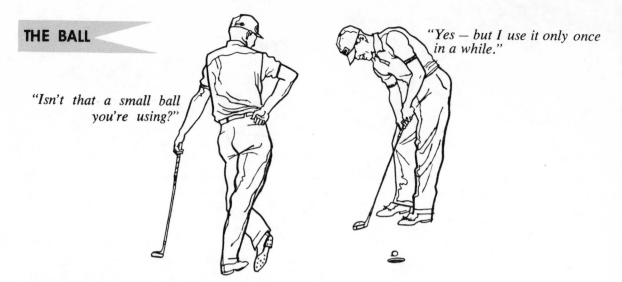

"Isn't that a small ball you're using?"

"Yes — but I use it only once in a while."

The weight of the ball shall be *not greater* than 1.620 ounces avoirdupois, and the size *not less* than 1.680 inches in diameter.

PENALTY: *Disqualification*. **Rule 2-3.**

MAXIMUM OF FOURTEEN CLUBS

"Let's be sure I have only fourteen clubs."

The player shall start a stipulated round with not more than fourteen clubs. He is limited to the clubs thus selected for that round except that, without unduly delaying play, he may:

a. If he started with fewer than fourteen, add as many as will bring his total to that number;
b. Replace, with any club, a club which becomes unfit for play in the normal course of play.

The addition or replacement of a club or clubs may not be made by borrowing from any other person playing on the course. PENALTY: *Match Play — Loss of one hole for each hole at which any violation occurred; maximum penalty per round; loss of two holes. The penalty shall be applied to the state of the match at the conclusion of the hole at which the violation is discovered, provided all players in the match have not left the putting green of the last hole of the match.*

Stroke play—Two strokes for each hole at which any violation occurred; maximum penalty per round: four strokes. **Rule 3-1.**

Wrong Club Declared Out of Play

Any club carried or used in violation of this Rule shall be declared out of play by the player immediately upon discovery and thereafter shall not be used by the player during the round. PENALTY: *Disqualification*. **Rule 3-3.**

AGREEMENT TO WAIVE RULES PROHIBITED

"Shall we play distance only for out of bounds?"

"No, indeed. We'll play by the Rules of Golf."

Players shall not agree to exclude the operation of any Rule or Local Rule or to waive any penalty incurred. PENALTY: *Match play — Disqualification of both sides; Stroke play — Disqualification of competitors concerned.* **Rule 4.**

GENERAL PENALTY

"There's no penalty given for breaking that Local Rule."

Except when otherwise provided for, the penalty for a breach of a Rule or Local Rule is: *Match play — Loss of hole; Stroke play — Two strokes.* **Rule 5.**

[23]

MATCH PLAY

9-Hole Match

HOLE	1	2	3	4	5	6	7	8	9	OUT
FRANK	5	5	3	3	4	4	4			
BOBBY	4	4	2	3	4	4	4			

Bobby winner of match 3 up and 2 to play

Holes Won   Holes Halved

1. Winner of Hole

In match play the game is played by holes.

Except as otherwise provided for in the Rules, a hole is won by the side which holes its ball in the fewer strokes. In a handicap match the lower net score wins the hole. **Rule 6-1.**

2. Halved Hole

A hole is halved if each side holes out in the same number of strokes. **Rule 6-2.**

3. Winner of Match

A match (which consists of a stipulated round, unless otherwise decreed by the Committee) is won by the side which is leading by a number of holes greater than the number of holes remaining to be played. **Rule 6-3.**

STROKE PLAY

HOLE	OUT	10	11	12	13	14	15	16	17	18	IN	TOTAL
FRANK	38	5	3	3	4	5	4	3	4	5	36	74
BOBBY	35	5	4	4	4	5	5	3	4	3	37	72

Bobby is the winner

The competitor who holes the stipulated round or rounds in the fewest strokes is the winner. **Rule 7-1.**

STROKE PLAY: FAILURE TO HOLE OUT

"No! This is stroke play. You must hole out."

"This is a gimme."

In stroke play, if a competitor fail to hole out at any hole before he has played a stroke from the next teeing ground, or, in the case of the last hole of the round, before he has left the putting green, he shall be disqualified. **Rule 7-2.**

(Ball purposely moved, touched or lifted—see Rules 27-1c and 35-1k.)

[24]

Mr. B is preparing to play his 4th stroke.

Mr. A, who has holed out in 4, says to Mr. B, "Your putt is going to break to the left."

Match play: If a player gives advice to his opponent, the player shall lose the hole. **Rule 9-1a.**

...BUT...

When a player has holed out (Mr. A in this case) and his opponent (Mr. B) has been left with a stroke for the half, nothing that the player who has holed out can do shall deprive him of the half which he has already gained; but if the player thereafter incur any penalty, the hole is halved. **Rule 6-2.**

"Watch out, Hank; I'm playing another shot for practice."

During the play of a hole, a player shall not play any practice stroke.
PENALTY: *Match play—Loss of hole; Stroke play—Two strokes.* **Rule 8-1.**

PRACTICE BETWEEN HOLES

"As long as we have to wait, don't you think it would be all right if we tried a few practice putts on the 9th green?"

"Can't do it — it's against the Rules."

Between the play of two holes, a player shall not play a practice stroke from any hazard, or on or to a putting green other than that of the hole last played. PENALTY: *Match play — Loss of hole (the penalty applies to the next hole); Stroke play — Two strokes*. **Rule 8-2.**

PRACTICE BEFORE STARTING OR BETWEEN ROUNDS

1st hole

Match Play: Unless otherwise decided by the Committee, there is no penalty for practice on the course on any day of a match play competition. **Rule 8-3, Note 2.**

Stroke Play: On any day of a stroke competition or play-off, a competitor shall not practice on the competition course before a round or play-off. When a competition extends over consecutive days, practice on the competition course between rounds is prohibited.
PENALTY: *Disqualification.* **Rule 8-3.**

[26]

*"Fine shot.
What club did you use?"*

A player may give advice to, or ask for advice from, only his partner or either of their caddies. In making a stroke, a player shall not seek or accept physical assistance or protection from the elements. PENALTY: *Match play—Loss of hole; Stroke play —Two strokes.* **Rule 9-1a, 1b.**

INDICATING LINE OF PLAY

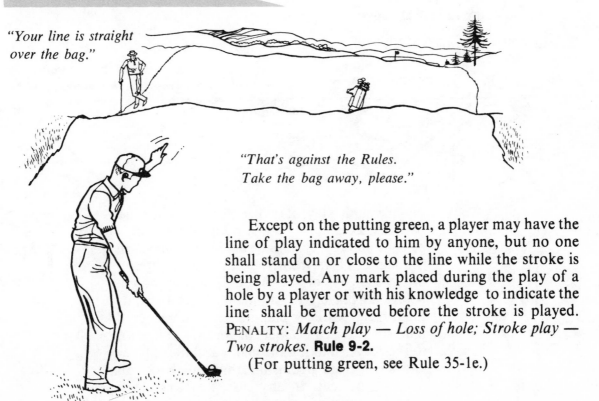

"Your line is straight over the bag."

*"That's against the Rules.
Take the bag away, please."*

Except on the putting green, a player may have the line of play indicated to him by anyone, but no one shall stand on or close to the line while the stroke is being played. Any mark placed during the play of a hole by a player or with his knowledge to indicate the line shall be removed before the stroke is played. PENALTY: *Match play — Loss of hole; Stroke play — Two strokes.* **Rule 9-2.**

(For putting green, see Rule 35-1e.)

"I lie 5, and not 4 as I said before you played your last shot. I forgot to include a penalty on my second shot. Sorry."

Match Play: A player who has incurred a penalty shall inform his opponent as soon as possible. If he fail to do so, he shall be deemed to have given wrong information. The number of strokes a player has taken shall include any penalty strokes incurred. **Rules 10-1 and 10-2.**

An opponent is entitled to ascertain from the player, during the play of a hole, the number of strokes he has taken. If during the play of a hole the player give wrong information as to the number of strokes taken, he shall incur no penalty if he correct the mistake before his opponent has played his next stroke. If the player fail to so correct the wrong information, he shall lose the hole. **Rule 10-2.**

CLAIMS IN MATCH PLAY

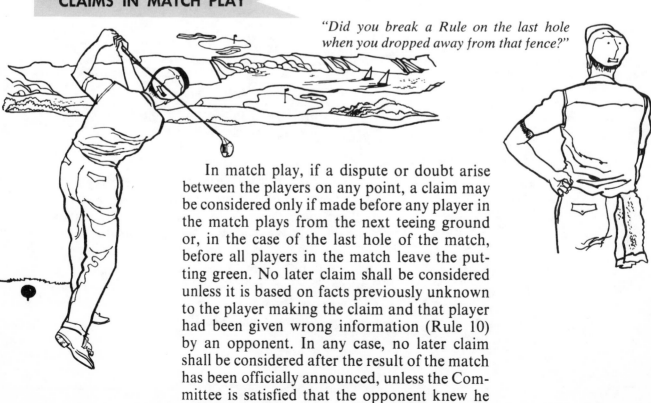

"Did you break a Rule on the last hole when you dropped away from that fence?"

In match play, if a dispute or doubt arise between the players on any point, a claim may be considered only if made before any player in the match plays from the next teeing ground or, in the case of the last hole of the match, before all players in the match leave the putting green. No later claim shall be considered unless it is based on facts previously unknown to the player making the claim and that player had been given wrong information (Rule 10) by an opponent. In any case, no later claim shall be considered after the result of the match has been officially announced, unless the Committee is satisfied that the opponent knew he was giving wrong information. **Rule 11-1.**

In stroke play only, when during play of a hole a competitor is doubtful of his rights or procedure, he may, without penalty, play a second ball. After the doubtful situation has arisen and before taking further action, he should announce to his marker his decision to proceed under this Rule and which ball he will score with if the Rules permit.

On completing the round, the competitor must report the facts immediately to the Committee; if he fail to do so, *he shall be disqualified*. If the Rules allow the procedure selected in advance by the competitor, the score with the ball selected shall be his score for the hole. Should the competitor fail to announce in advance his procedure or selection, the ball with the higher score shall count if the Rules allow the procedure adopted for such ball. **Rule 11-5.**

THE TEEING GROUND

THE HONOR — PLAYING OUT OF TURN

"I believe it was my honor."

Match Play

If, on the teeing ground, a player play when his opponent should have played, the opponent may immediately require the player to abandon the ball so played and to play a ball in correct order, without penalty.

Stroke Play

If, on the teeing ground, a competitor by mistake play out of turn, no penalty shall be incurred and the ball shall be in play.

Rule 12-2a, 2b.

THE HONOR — SECOND BALL FROM TEE

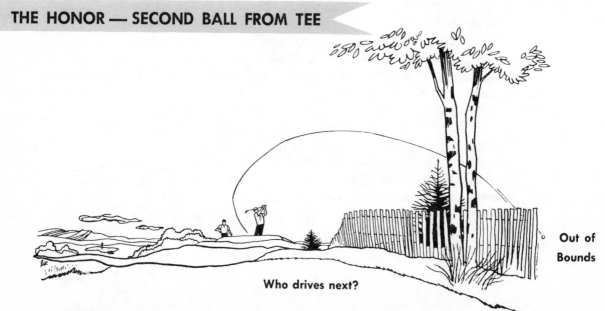

Out of
Bounds

Who drives next?

If a player play a second ball, including a provisional ball, from the tee, he should do so after the opponent or the fellow-competitor has played his first stroke. **Rule 12-2c.**

PLAYING OUTSIDE TEEING GROUND

Stance legal **Ball's position wrong**

Match Play

If a player, when starting a hole, play a ball from outside the teeing ground, the opponent may immediately require the player to replay the stroke, in which case the player shall tee a ball and play the stroke from within the teeing ground, without penalty. **Rule 13-1.**

Stroke Play

If a competitor, when starting a hole, play from outside the teeing ground, he shall be penalized two strokes and shall then play from within the teeing ground. Strokes played by a competitor from outside the teeing ground do not count in his score. If the competitor fail to rectify his mistake before making a stroke on the next teeing ground, or, in the case of the last hole of the round, before leaving the putting green, he shall be disqualified. **Rule 13-2.**

NOTE: *Stance.* A player may take his stance outside the teeing ground to play a ball within it.

BALL FALLING OFF TEE

If a ball, when not in play, fall off a tee or be knocked off a tee by the player in addressing it, it may be re-teed without penalty, but if a stroke be made at the ball in these circumstances, whether the ball be moving or not, the stroke shall be counted but no penalty shall be incurred. **Rule 14.**

[31]

MIXED FOURSOME

The lady has hit the ball into the water hazard and the man is dropping a ball behind the hazard under penalty of one stroke (Rule 33-2a). Who should play the next stroke, the man or his lady partner?

The man should play the next stroke because a penalty stroke does not affect the order of play.

General   In a threesome or a foursome, the partners strike off alternately from the teeing grounds, and thereafter shall strike alternately during the play of each hole. Penalty strokes (Definition 24) do not affect the order of play. **Rule 15-1**.

Match Play   If a player play when his partner should have played, his side shall lose the hole. **Rule 15-2**.

Stroke Play   If the partners play a stroke or strokes in incorrect order, such stroke or strokes shall be cancelled, and the side shall be penalized two strokes. A ball shall then be put in play as nearly as possible at the spot from which the side first played in incorrect order. This must be done before a stroke has been played from the next teeing ground, or, in the case of the last hole of the round, before the side has left the putting green. If they fail to do so, they shall be disqualified. **Rule 15-3**.

BALL PLAYED AS IT LIES; EMBEDDED BALL

The ball shall be played as it lies except as otherwise provided in the Rules or Local Rules. **Rule 16-1**. (For ball moved, see Rule 27.)

A ball embedded in its own pitch-mark in any closely mown area through the green may be lifted and dropped, without penalty, as near as possible to the spot where it lay but not nearer the hole. **Rule 16-2**.

IMPROVING LIE PROHIBITED

The player is not of necessity entitled to see the ball when playing a stroke. If a ball lie in long grass, rushes, bushes, whins, heather or the like, only so much thereof shall be touched as will enable the player to find and identify his ball; nothing shall be done which may in any way improve its lie. PENALTY: *Match play — Loss of hole; Stroke play — Two strokes*. **Rule 17-2.**

Are you always allowed to see the ball when you play?

IMPROVING LINE OF PLAY OR LIE PROHIBITED

"Do you want me to hold back this limb?"

How hard may the player press down the grass?

A player shall not improve, or allow to be improved, his line of play, the position or lie of his ball or the area of his intended swing by moving, bending or breaking anything fixed or growing, or by removing or pressing down sand, loose soil, cut turf placed in position or other irregularities of surface except:

a. As may occur in the course of fairly taking his stance;
b. In making the stroke or the backward movement of his club for the stroke;
c. On the teeing ground, a player may create or eliminate irregularities of surface;
d. In repairing damage to the putting green under Rule 35-1c.

The club may be grounded only lightly and must not be pressed on the ground. PENALTY: *Match play—Loss of hole; Stroke play—Two strokes*. **Rule 17-1.**

[33]

BUILDING STANCE PROHIBITED

This is wrong

A player is always entitled to place his feet firmly on the ground when taking his stance, but he is not allowed to build a stance. PENALTY: *Match play — Loss of hole; Stroke play — Two strokes.* **Rule 17-3.**

LOOSE IMPEDIMENTS

May the twig be removed? Yes, but ... There's a penalty if the ball **moves**

Any loose impediment may be removed without penalty except when both the impediment and the ball lie in or touch a hazard. When a player's ball is in motion, a loose impediment on his line of play shall not be removed. PENALTY: *Match play — Loss of hole; Stroke play — Two strokes.* **Rule 18.**

(Finding ball in hazard—see Rule 33-le.)

Through the green, if the ball move before the player had addressed it but after any loose impediment lying within a club-length of it has been touched by the player, his partner or either of their caddies, the player shall be deemed to have caused the ball to move. The penalty shall be one stroke. The ball shall be replaced unless the movement of the ball occurs after the player has begun his swing and he does not discontinue his swing. **Rule 27-1e.**

(Loose impediments on putting green—see Rule 35-lb.)

STRIKING AT BALL FAIRLY

WRONG

The ball shall be fairly struck at with the head of the club and must not be pushed, scraped or spooned. PENALTY: *Match play — Loss of hole; Stroke play — Two strokes.* **Rule 19-1.**

STRIKING BALL TWICE

If the player strike the ball twice when making a stroke, he shall count the stroke and add a penalty stroke, making two strokes in all. **Rule 19-2.**

(Playing a moving ball — see Rule 25.)

General

When the balls are in play, the ball farther from the hole shall be played first. If the balls are equidistant from the hole, the option of playing first should be decided by lot. **Rule 20-1.**

Match Play

Through the green or in a hazard, if a player play when his opponent should have done so, the opponent may immediately require the player to replay the stroke. In such a case, the player shall drop a ball as near as possible to the spot from which his previous stroke was played, and play in correct order without penalty. PENALTY FOR BREACH OF RULE: *Loss of hole.* **Rule 20-2.**

(Playing out of turn on putting green—see Rule 35-2b.)

Stroke Play

If a competitor play out of turn, no penalty shall be incurred. The ball shall be played as it lies. **Rule 20-3.**

A player must hole out with the ball driven from the teeing ground unless a Rule or Local Rule permits him to substitute another ball. **Rule 21-1**.

If a player play a stroke with a wrong ball (Definition 5) except in a hazard:

Match Play

The player shall lose the hole. When the player and the opponent exchange balls, the first to play the wrong ball other than from a hazard shall lose the hole; when this cannot be determined, the hole shall be played out with the balls exchanged. **Rule 21-2a**.

Stroke Play

The player shall add two penalty strokes to his score for the hole and shall then play the correct ball (provided he has not made a stroke on the next teeing ground, or, in the case of the last hole of the round, has not left the putting green). Strokes played with a wrong ball do not count in his score. **Rule 21-3a**.

There is no penalty for a player playing a stroke or strokes in a hazard with a wrong ball provided he then play the correct ball, in match play and stroke play. Strokes played with a wrong ball do not count in his score. **Rule 21-2a, 3a**.

LIFTING, DROPPING AND PLACING

WHO MAY LIFT

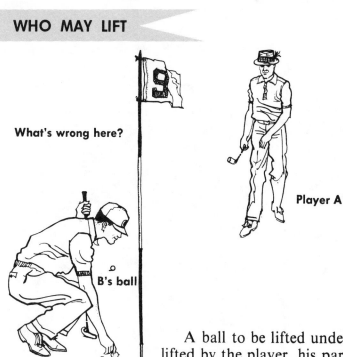

What's wrong here?

B's ball

Player A

Player B   A's ball

A ball to be lifted under the Rules or Local Rules may be lifted by the player, his partner, or another person authorized by the player. When a ball is lifted by someone else in the group without the authority of the ball's owner, the following apply:

Match play: If the ball is lifted by the opponent, the opponent incurs a penalty stroke, and the ball shall be replaced. **Rule 27-2a.** If the ball is lifted by the player's caddie, the player incurs a penalty stroke, and the ball shall be replaced. **Rule 27-1c.**

Stroke play: If the ball is lifted by a fellow-competitor or his caddie, no penalty is incurred. The competitor's ball shall be replaced. **Rule 27-3.** If the ball is lifted by the competitor's caddie, the competitor incurs a penalty stroke, and the ball shall be replaced. **Rule 27-1c.**

Rule 22-1.

HOW TO DROP

A ball to be dropped under the Rules or Local Rules shall be dropped by the player himself. He shall face the hole, stand erect, and drop the ball behind him over his shoulder. If the ball be dropped in any other manner and remain the ball in play (Definition 5), the player shall incur a penalty stroke. If the ball touch the player before it strikes the ground, the player shall re-drop without penalty. If the ball touch the player after it strikes the ground, or if it comes to rest against the player and moves when he then moves, there is no penalty, and the ball shall be played as it lies.

PENALTY FOR BREACH OF RULE: *Match play—Loss of hole; Stroke play—Two strokes.* **Rule 22-2a.**

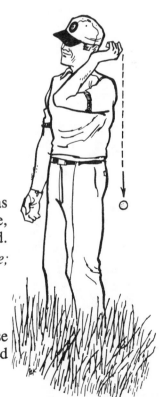

WHERE TO DROP

When a ball is to be dropped, it shall be dropped as near as possible to the spot where the ball lay, but not nearer the hole, except when a Rule permits it to be dropped elsewhere or placed.

PENALTY FOR BREACH OF RULE: *Match play — Loss of hole; Stroke play — Two strokes.* **Rule 22-2b.**

Ball in Play when Dropped
A ball dropped under a Rule governing the particular case is in play (Definition 5) and shall not be lifted or re-dropped except as provided in the Rules. **Rule 22-4.**

LIFTING, DROPPING AND PLACING

When a ball is to be dropped in a hazard, it must come to rest in that hazard; if it roll out of the hazard, it must be re-dropped, without penalty. PENALTY FOR BREACH OF RULE: *Match play — Loss of hole; Stroke play — Two strokes.*

Rule 22-2b.

DROPPED BALL ROLLING INTO NEW SITUATION

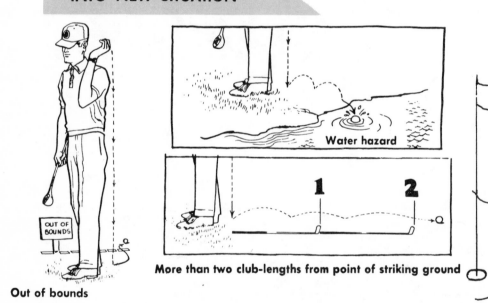

Water hazard

1 **2**

More than two club-lengths from point of striking ground

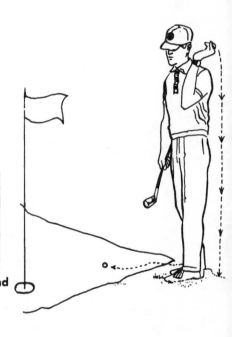

OUT OF BOUNDS

Out of bounds

If a dropped ball roll into a hazard, onto a putting green, out of bounds, or more than two club-lengths from the point where it first struck the ground, or come to rest nearer the hole than its original position, it shall be re-dropped, without penalty. If the ball again roll into such a position, it shall be placed where it first struck the ground when re-dropped. **Rule 22-2c.**

PENALTY FOR BREACH OF RULE 22-2: *Match play — Loss of hole; Stroke play — Two strokes.*

[40]

HOW AND WHERE TO PLACE

A ball to be placed under the Rules or Local Rules shall be placed by the player or his partner. A ball to be replaced shall be replaced by the player, his partner or the person who lifted it, on the spot where the ball lay. **Rule 22-3a.**

Spot not Determinable

If it be impossible to determine the spot where the ball is to be placed, through the green or in a hazard the ball shall be dropped, or on the putting green it shall be placed, as near as possible to the place where it lay but not nearer the hole. **Rule 22-3c.**

Ball Moving

If a ball when placed fail to remain on the spot on which it was placed, it shall be replaced without penalty. If it still fail to remain on that spot, it shall be placed at the nearest spot not nearer the hole where it can be placed at rest. **Rule 22-3d.**

PENALTY FOR BREACH OF RULE: *Match play — Loss of hole; Stroke play — Two strokes.*

Ball in Play when Placed

A ball placed under a Rule governing the particular case is in play (Definition 5) and shall not be lifted or re-dropped or replaced except as provided in the Rules. **Rule 22-4.**

LIE OF BALL TO BE PLACED OR REPLACED ALTERED

"Please lift your ball. It interferes with me."

Player A

A's ball

B's ball

Player B

B's lie is altered

Player B

If the original lie of a ball to be placed or replaced has been altered, the ball shall be placed in the nearest lie most similar to that which it originally occupied, not more than two club-lengths from the original lie and not nearer the hole. **Rule 22-3b.**

PENALTY FOR BREACH OF RULE 22-3b: *Match play — Loss of hole; Stroke play — Two strokes.*

LIFTING, DROPPING AND PLACING

LIFTING BALL WRONGLY DROPPED OR PLACED

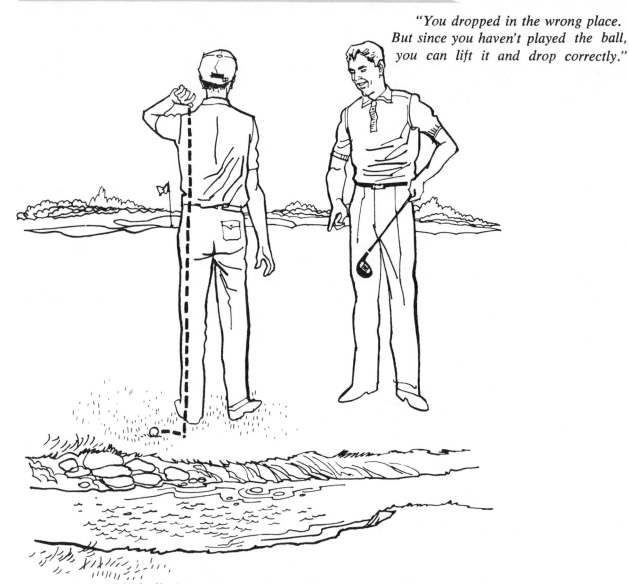

"You dropped in the wrong place. But since you haven't played the ball, you can lift it and drop correctly."

A ball dropped or placed but not played may be lifted without penalty if:

a. It was dropped or placed under a Rule governing the particular case but not in the right place or otherwise not in accordance with that Rule. The player shall then drop or place the ball in accordance with the governing Rule.

b. It was dropped or placed under a Rule which does not govern the particular case. The player shall then proceed under a Rule which governs the case. However, in match play, if, before the opponent plays his next stroke, the player fail to inform him that the ball has been lifted, the player shall lose the hole. **Rule 22-5.**

[42]

IDENTIFYING OR CLEANING BALL

IDENTIFICATION MARK ON BALL

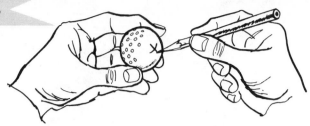

The responsibility for playing the proper ball rests with the player. Each player should put an identification mark on his ball.

Rule 23, Preamble.

LIFTING FOR IDENTIFICATION

May he lift the ball?

Yes

No

Sand in bunker

Except in a hazard, the player may, without penalty, lift his ball in play for the purpose of identification and replace it on the spot from which it was lifted provided this is done in the presence of his opponent in match play or his marker in stroke play. If the player lift his ball for identification in a hazard, or elsewhere other than in the presence of his opponent or marker, he shall incur a penalty of one stroke, and the ball shall be replaced. **Rule 23-1.**

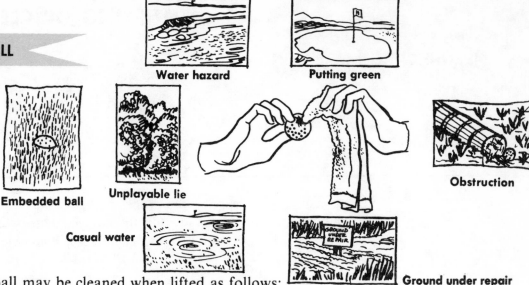

Water hazard

Putting green

Embedded ball

Unplayable lie

Casual water

Obstruction

Ground under repair

A ball may be cleaned when lifted as follows:

From an embedded lie under Rule 16-2;

From an unplayable lie under Rule 29-2;

For relief from an obstruction under Rule 31;

From casual water, ground under repair or otherwise under Rule 32;

From a water hazard under Rule 33-2 or 33-3;

On the putting green under Rule 35-1d or on a wrong putting green under Rule 35-1j.

For identification under Rule 23-1, but the ball may be cleaned only to the extent necessary for identification; or

Under a Local Rule permitting cleaning of the ball.

If the player clean his ball during the play of a hole except as permitted under this Rule, he shall incur a penalty of one stroke and the ball if lifted shall be replaced. **Rule 23-2.**

BALL INTERFERING WITH PLAY

When the player's ball lies through the green or in a hazard, the player may have any other ball lifted if he consider that it interfere with his play. A ball so lifted shall be replaced after the player has played his stroke.

If a ball be accidentally moved in complying with this Rule, no penalty shall be incurred and the ball shall be replaced.

PENALTY FOR BREACH: *Match play — Loss of hole; Stroke play — Two strokes.*

Rule 24.

(Lie of ball to be placed or replaced altered—Rule 22-3b.)

(Putting green—Rule 35-2a and 35-3a.)

B's ball

Player B

A's ball

Player A

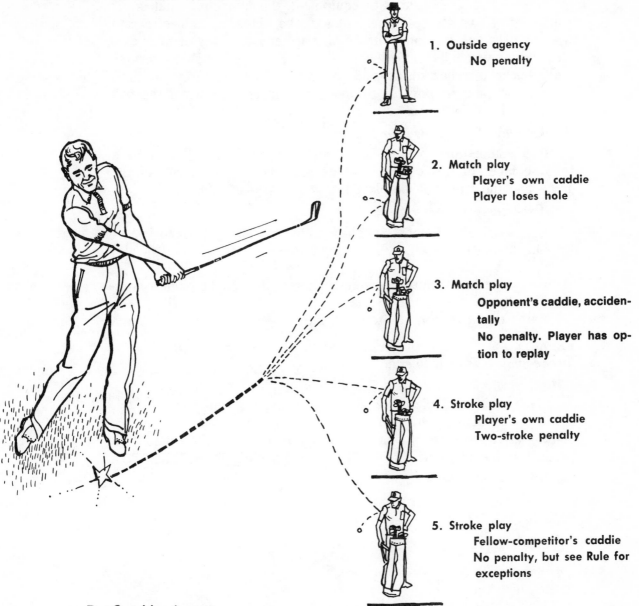

1. Outside agency
   No penalty

2. Match play
   Player's own caddie
   Player loses hole

3. Match play
   Opponent's caddie, accidentally
   No penalty. Player has option to replay

4. Stroke play
   Player's own caddie
   Two-stroke penalty

5. Stroke play
   Fellow-competitor's caddie
   No penalty, but see Rule for exceptions

By Outside Agency

If a ball in motion be accidentally stopped or deflected by any outside agency, it is a rub of the green and the ball shall be played as it lies, without penalty. **Rule 26-1a.**

Exception: On putting green—Rule 35-1h.

Match Play: By Player

If a player's ball be stopped or deflected by himself, his partner or either of their caddies or equipment, he shall lose the hole. **Rule 26-2a.**

Match Play: By Opponent, Accidentally

If a player's ball be accidentally stopped or deflected by an opponent, his caddie or equipment, no penalty shall be incurred. The player may play the ball as it lies or, before another stroke is played by either side, he may cancel the stroke, place a ball on the spot where the ball previously lay and replay the stroke.

Exception:—Ball striking person attending flagstick—Rule 34-3b.

(Ball purposely stopped or deflected by opponent—Rule 17-4.)

(Ball striking opponent's ball—Rule 27-2b.)

Stroke Play: By Competitor

If a competitor's ball be stopped or deflected by himself, his partner or either of their caddies or equipment, the competitor shall incur a penalty of two strokes. The ball shall be played as it lies, except when it lodges in the competitor's, his partner's or either of their caddies' clothes or equipment, in which case the competitor shall, through the green or in a hazard, drop the ball, or on the putting green place the ball, as near as possible to where the article was when the ball lodged in it. **Rule 26-3a.**

Stroke Play: By Fellow-Competitor

If a competitor's ball be accidentally stopped or deflected by a fellow-competitor, his caddie, ball or equipment, it is a rub of the green and the ball shall be played as it lies. **Rule 26-3b.**

Exceptions:

Ball lodging in fellow-competitor's clothes, etc. — Rule 26-1b.
On the putting green, ball striking fellow-competitor's ball in play
   —Rule 35-3c.
Ball played from putting green stopped or deflected by fellow-competitor or his caddie—Rule 35-1h.
Ball striking person attending flagstick — Rule 34-3b.

PENALTY FOR BREACH OF RULE: *Match play — Loss of hole;*
Stroke play — Two strokes.

Deliberate Deflection

NOTE: If the referee or the Committee determine that a ball has been deliberately stopped or deflected by an outside agency, including a fellow-competitor or his caddie, further procedure should be prescribed in equity under Rule 11-4. On the putting green, Rule 35-1h applies.

Playing a moving ball is prohibited . . .   **. . . but . . .**

IN
WATER HAZARD

A player shall not play while his ball is moving.

PENALTY: *Match play — Loss of hole;
Stroke play — Two strokes.* **Rule 25-1**.

. . . but . . .

When the ball only begins to move after the player has begun the stroke or the backward movement of his club for the stroke, he shall incur no penalty under Rule 25-1 for playing a moving ball. However, he is not exempted from penalty if his ball moved:

After removal of a loose impediment (see Rule 27-1e);
Accidentally due to the player's action (see Rule 27-1d);
After it had been addressed (see Rule 27-1f).

Rule 25-1.

When a ball is in water in a water hazard, the player may, without penalty, make a stroke at it while it is moving, but he must not delay to make his stroke in order to allow the wind or current to better the position of the ball. A ball moving in water in a water hazard may be lifted if the player elect to invoke Rule 33-2 or 33-3. PENALTY: *Match play — Loss of hole; Stroke play — Two strokes.*

Rule 25-2.

[47]

BALL AT REST MOVED

"Drop that ball.

If a ball at rest be moved by any outside agency, the player shall incur no penalty and shall replace the ball before playing another stroke.

Note 1: Neither wind nor water is an outside agency.

Note 2: If the ball moved is not immediately recoverable, another ball may be substituted.

Rule 27-1a.

DURING SEARCH; BY PLAYER OR HIS CADDIE ACCIDENTALLY

Player B — Player A — *"Sorry, Mr. B — I guess I kicked your ball."* — B's ball

"Gosh, Mr. A — I moved your ball. That's a penalty." — Caddie A — A's ball

During search for a ball, if it be moved by an opponent, a fellow-competitor or the equipment or caddie of either, no penalty shall be incurred. The player shall replace the ball before playing another stroke. **Rule 27-1b.**

When a ball is in play, if a player, his partner, their equipment or either of their caddies accidentally move it, or by touching anything cause it to move, except as provided for in the Rules, the player shall incur a penalty stroke. The ball shall be replaced unless the movement of the ball occurs after the player has begun his swing and he does not discontinue his swing. **Rule 27-1d.**

When a ball is in play, if a player, his partner or either of their caddies purposely move, touch or lift it, except as provided for in the Rules or Local Rules, the player shall incur a penalty stroke and the ball shall be replaced. The player may, however, without penalty, touch the ball with his club in the act of addressing it, provided the ball does not move. **Rule 27-1c.**

If the player fail to replace the ball, he incurs a penalty of loss of hole in match play or an additional penalty of two strokes in stroke play. **Note 1 to Rule 27.**

(On putting green—Rule 35-1k.)

"You shouldn't have lifted my ball out of the divot."

BALL MOVING ACCIDENTALLY AFTER ADDRESS

If a ball in play move after the player has addressed it (Definition 1), he shall be deemed to have caused it to move and shall incur a penalty stroke, and the ball shall be played as it lies.

Rule 27-1f.

BALL AT REST MOVED

BALL MOVED BY ANOTHER SIDE

"Hey, you kicked my ball."

Player A

Player B

B's ball

Match Play

If a player's ball be touched or moved by an opponent, his caddie or his equipment (except as otherwise provided in the Rules), the opponent shall incur a penalty stroke. The player shall replace the ball before playing another stroke. **Rule 27-2a.**

Stroke Play

If a competitor's ball be moved by a fellow-competitor, his caddie, ball or equipment, no penalty shall be incurred. The competitor shall replace his ball before playing another stroke. **Rule 27-3.**

Exception to penalty: Ball striking fellow-competitor's ball on putting green—Rule 35-3c.

OPPONENT'S BALL MOVED BY PLAYER'S BALL

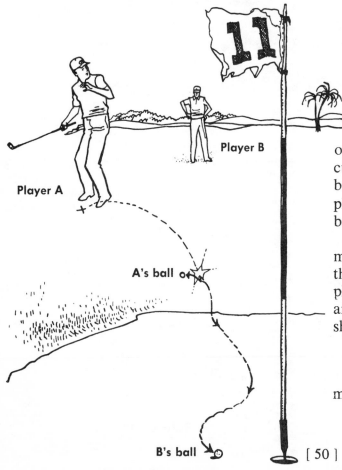

Player A

Player B

A's ball

B's ball

Match Play: If a player's ball move an opponent's ball, no penalty shall be incurred. The opponent may either play his ball as it lies or, before another stroke is played by either side, he may replace the ball.

If the player's ball stop on the spot formerly occupied by the opponent's ball and the opponent declare his intention to replace the ball, the player shall first play another stroke, after which the opponent shall replace his ball. **Rule 27-2b.**

(Putting green — Rule 35-2c.)

(Three-Ball, Best-Ball and Four-Ball match play — Rule 40-1c.)

[50]

"I'm going to play this cut ball on this water hole."

"Then you can't change the ball on the green."

The ball may be deemed unfit for play when it is visibly cut or out of shape or so cracked, pierced or otherwise damaged as to interfere with its true flight or true roll or its normal behavior when struck. The ball shall not be deemed unfit for play solely because mud or other material adheres to it, its surface be scratched or its paint be damaged or discolored.

If a player has reason to believe his ball is unfit for play, the player, after he has announced his intention to proceed under this Rule to his opponent in match play or marker in stroke play, may, without penalty, lift his ball in play for the purpose of determining whether it is unfit. If the ball is so damaged as to be unfit for play, the player may substitute another ball, placing it on the spot where the original ball lay. Substitution may only be made on the hole during the play in which the damage occurred.

If a ball break into pieces as a result of a stroke, a ball shall be placed where the original ball lay and the stroke shall be replayed, without penalty.

A player is not the sole judge as to whether his ball is unfit for play. If the opponent or the marker dispute a claim of unfitness, the referee, if one is present, or the Committee shall settle the matter (Rule 11-2 or 11-3).

PENALTY FOR BREACH OF RULE: *Match play — Loss of hole; Stroke play — Two strokes.*

(Ball unplayable — Rule 29-2.)

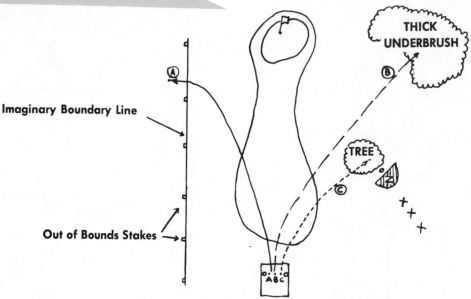

Imaginary Boundary Line

THICK UNDERBRUSH

TREE

Out of Bounds Stakes

Out of Bounds   Player A's ball is out of bounds. He must replay from the tee, count both strokes made and add a penalty stroke to his score for the hole. **Rule 29-1a.**

Lost   Player B is unable to find his ball in the thick underbrush. His only procedure for a lost ball is to play again from the tee, count both strokes played and add a penalty stroke to his score for the hole. **Rule 29-1a.**

Unplayable   Player C finds his ball at the base of a thick, bushy tree. He declares it unplayable under Rule 29-2a (the player may declare it unplayable at any place on the course except in a water hazard). He has three options for relief:

1. He may play again from the tee, under the same procedure and penalty as did A and B; or
2. He may drop a ball, under penalty of one stroke, either:
   (a) Within two club-lengths of the point where the ball lay, but not nearer the hole (shaded area Z), or
   (b) Behind the unplayable lie on line XXX so as to keep the point where the ball lies unplayable between himself and the hole, with no limit to how far behind that point the ball may be dropped. (If the ball lie in a bunker and Player C elect to proceed under option 2(a) or 2(b), he would have to drop in the bunker.)

Rule 29-2b.

(Ball in casual water, etc.—Rule 32.)

(Ball unfit for play — Rule 28.)

PENALTY FOR BREACH OF RULE: *Match play — Loss of hole; Stroke play — Two strokes.*

WHEN PROVISIONAL BALL PERMITTED

OUT OF BOUNDS

THICK UNDERBRUSH

POND

"That may be lost or out of bounds. I'll play a provisional."

"That could be in the pond or unplayable under a tree. Is a provisional allowed?"

"Sorry — not for those reasons."

If a ball may be lost outside a water hazard or may be out of bounds, to save time the player may play another ball provisionally as nearly as possible from the spot at which the original ball was played. If the original ball was played from the teeing ground, the provisional ball may be teed anywhere within the teeing ground; if from through the green or a hazard, it shall be dropped; if on the putting green, it shall be placed.

The player must inform his opponent or marker that he intends to play a provisional ball, and he must play it before he or his partner goes forward to search for the original ball. If he fail to do so, and play another ball, such ball is not a provisional ball and becomes the ball in play under penalty of stroke and distance (Rule 29-1); the original ball is deemed to be lost (Definition 6b).

PENALTY FOR BREACH OF RULE: *Match play — Loss of hole; Stroke play — Two strokes.* **Rule 30-1.**

(A Local Rule may allow a provisional ball for a ball which may be in a water hazard of such character that it would be impracticable to determine whether the ball is in the hazard or to do so would unduly delay play. See Appendix I.)

PROVISIONAL BALL

"That puts the provisional ball in play."

"That's unplayable. I'll have to give up the provisional ball, too."

Original ball

Provisional ball

OUT OF BOUNDS

Original ball

Provisional ball

The player may play a provisional ball until he reaches the place where the original ball is likely to be. If he play any strokes with the provisional ball from a point nearer the hole than that place, the original ball is deemed to be lost (Definition 6c).

If the original ball be lost outside a water hazard or be out of bounds, the provisional ball becomes the ball in play, under penalty of stroke and distance (Rule 29-1).

If the original ball be neither lost outside a water hazard nor out of bounds, the player shall abandon the provisional ball and continue play with the original ball. Should he fail to do so, any further strokes played with the provisional ball shall constitute playing a wrong ball and the provisions of Rule 21 shall apply.

Rule 30-2.

PENALTY FOR BREACH OF RULE: *Match play — Loss of hole; Stroke play — Two strokes.*

NOTE: If the original ball be unplayable or lie or be lost in a water hazard, the player must proceed under Rule 29-2 or Rule 33-2 or 33-3, whichever is applicable.

Any movable obstruction may be removed. If the ball be moved in so doing, it shall be replaced on the exact spot from which it was moved, without penalty. If it be impossible to determine the spot or to replace the ball, the player shall proceed in accordance with Rule 22-3.

When a ball is in motion, an obstruction on the player's line of play other than an attended flagstick and equipment of the players shall not be moved.

PENALTY FOR BREACH OF RULE: *Match play — Loss of hole; Stroke play — Two strokes.* **Rule 31-1.**

IMMOVABLE OBSTRUCTIONS

Interference by an immovable obstruction occurs when the ball lies in or on the obstruction, or so close to the obstruction that the obstruction interferes with the player's stance or the area of his intended swing. A player may obtain relief from interference by an immovable obstruction, without penalty, as follows:

a. *Through the green,* the point nearest to where the ball lies shall be determined (without crossing over, through or under the obstruction) which (a) is not nearer the hole, (b) avoids interference as defined in Clause 2a of this Rule, and (c) is not in a hazard or on a putting green. He shall lift the ball and drop it within one club-length of the point thus determined on ground which fulfils (a), (b) and (c) above.

NOTE: The prohibition against crossing over, through or under the obstruction does not apply to the artificial surfaces and sides of roads and paths or when the ball lies in or on the obstruction.

b. *In a hazard,* the player may lift and drop the ball in accordance with Clause *a* above, except that the ball must be dropped in the hazard.

c. *On the putting green,* the player may lift and place the ball in the nearest position to where it lay which affords relief from interference, but not nearer the hole.

PENALTY FOR BREACH OF RULE: *Match play — Loss of hole; Stroke play — Two strokes.* **Rule 31-2.**

OBSTRUCTIONS

RELIEF FROM PAVED CART PATH

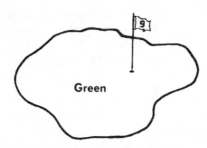

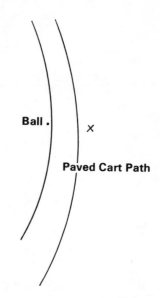

The ball is in such position that the paved cart path (an obstruction) interferes with the player's stance. Although Rule 31-2 (page 55) in general prohibits crossing over the obstruction in determining the nearest point of relief, the prohibition does not apply to paved paths — see Note to Rule 31-2. Thus, the player, if he desires relief, must drop the ball within one club-length of point X, the nearest point of relief not nearer the hole.

NO RELIEF FOR LINE OF PLAY ALONE

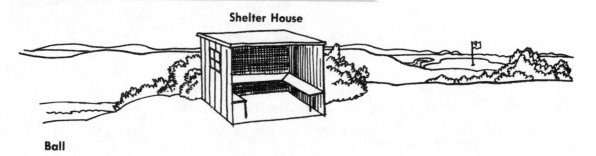

The ball lies so far behind the shelter house that it does not interfere with the player's swing. The player is not entitled to drop his ball so as to avoid the shelter house on line to the green. Rule 31-2a provides that intervention on the line of play is not, of itself, interference under this Rule.

CASUAL WATER, GROUND UNDER REPAIR

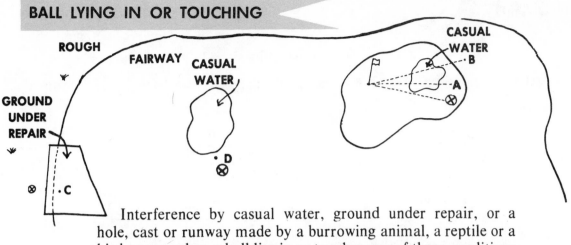

Interference by casual water, ground under repair, or a hole, cast or runway made by a burrowing animal, a reptile or a bird occurs when a ball lies in or touches any of these conditions or when the condition interferes with the player's stance or the area of the intended swing. If interference exists, the player may either play the ball as it lies or take relief as follows:

On the Putting Green

Ball A lies on the putting green with casual water intervening to the hole. *Ball A* may be lifted without penalty and placed at nearby point X, which is the nearest position to where it lay which affords maximum relief from the casual water, but not nearer the hole. If *Ball A* were lying *in* casual water on the putting green, similar relief would be available. **Rule 32-3c.**

Ball B lies off the putting green. The player is not entitled to relief from casual water lying on the putting green which intervenes between *Ball B* and the hole.

Through the Green

Ball C lies in ground under repair, in an area normally "fairway." *Ball C* may be lifted and dropped without penalty outside the ground under repair within one club-length of X, the nearest point which (a) is not nearer the hole, (b) avoids interference by the condition, and (c) is not in a hazard or on a putting green. **Rule 32-3a.** (The permissible drop area is in the "rough," but the Rules do not distinguish between "fairway" and "rough" — both are "through the green," according to Definition 35.)

Ball D lies so near to casual water that a right-handed player would be obliged to stand in casual water. He may lift and drop the ball without penalty outside the casual water, within one club-length of the nearest point of relief not nearer the hole. The point is indicated by the X.

PENALTY FOR BREACH OF RULE: *Match play — Loss of hole; Stroke play — Two strokes.*

CASUAL WATER, GROUND UNDER REPAIR

IN A HAZARD

CASUAL WATER IN BUNKER

Area W — water 3 inches deep; *Area X* — water ⅛ inch deep; *Area Y* — no casual water.

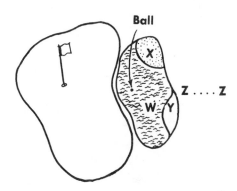 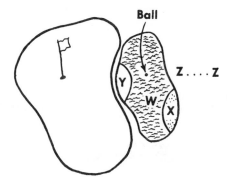

I. The player would like to drop the ball in area X. However, he may drop only:

1. At nearest point in area Y, without penalty, or

2. Along line Z . . . Z behind the bunker, under penalty of one stroke.

II. The player may drop the ball at either:

1. The nearest point in area X, without penalty, or

2. Along line Z . . . Z behind the bunker, under penalty of one stroke. He may not drop in area Y as it is nearer the hole than the ball's original position.

In a hazard, if there is interference by casual water, ground under repair, or a hole, cast or runway made by a burrowing animal, a reptile or a bird, the player may lift and drop the ball either:

> Without penalty, in the hazard as near as possible to the spot where the ball lay, but not nearer the hole, on ground which affords maximum relief from the condition;

or

> Under penalty of one stroke, outside the hazard, but not nearer the hole, keeping the spot where the ball lay between himself and the hole.

PENALTY FOR BREACH OF RULE: *Match play — Loss of hole; Stroke play — Two strokes.*

Rule 32-3b.

CASUAL WATER, GROUND UNDER REPAIR

"I'm sure my ball went in here, but I can't find it."

In order that a ball may be treated as lost under a condition covered by Rule 32, there must be reasonable evidence to that effect. If a ball be lost under such condition through the green, the player may take relief as follows: the point nearest to where the ball last crossed the margin of the area shall be determined which (a) is not nearer the hole than where the ball last crossed that margin, (b) avoids interference by the condition, and (c) is not in a hazard or on a putting green. He shall drop a ball without penalty within one club-length of the point thus determined on ground which fulfils (a), (b) and (c) above. **Rule 32-4.**

PENALTY FOR BREACH OF RULE: *Match play — Loss of hole; Stroke play — Two strokes.*

HAZARDS

When a ball lies in or touches a hazard or a water hazard, nothing shall be done which may in any way improve its lie. Before making a stroke, the player shall not touch the ground in the hazard or water in the water hazard with a club or otherwise, nor touch or move a loose impediment lying in or touching the hazard, nor test the condition of the hazard or of any similar hazard; subject to the following considerations among others:

Touching Fixed or Growing Object

In addressing the ball or in the stroke or in the backward movement for the stroke, the club may touch any wooden or stone wall, paling or similar fixed object or any grass, bush, tree, or other growing substance (but the club may not be soled in the hazard).

PENALTY FOR BREACH OF RULE: *Match play — Loss of hole; Stroke play — Two strokes.* **Rule 33-1.**

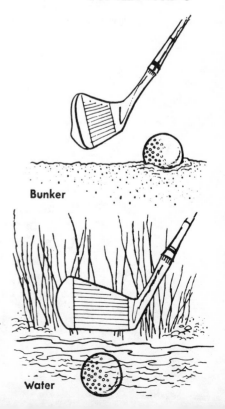

Bunker

Water

[59]

HAZARDS

LOOSE IMPEDIMENTS AND OBSTRUCTIONS

Loose impediments must not be touched
Rule 33-1

Obstructions may be removed
Rule 33-1c

FINDING BALL

"I'm sure the ball is here someplace."

"My ball must be buried in the sand."

In a hazard, if the ball be covered by sand, fallen leaves or the like, the player may remove as much thereof as will enable him to see the top of the ball; if the ball be moved in such removal, no penalty shall be incurred, and the ball shall be replaced.

If the ball is believed to be lying in water in a water hazard, the player may probe for it with a club or otherwise. If the ball be moved in such search, no penalty shall be incurred; the ball shall be replaced, unless the player elects to proceed under Clause 2 or 3 of this Rule.

The ball may not be lifted for identification.

PENALTY FOR BREACH OF RULE: *Match play — Loss of hole; Stroke play — Two strokes.*

Rule 33-1e.

[60]

SMOOTHING IRREGULARITIES

Bunker

There is no penalty should soil or sand in the hazard be smoothed by the player after playing a stroke, or by his caddie at any time without the authority of the player, provided nothing is done that improves the lie of the ball or assists the player in his subsequent play of the hole.

PENALTY FOR BREACH OF RULE: *Match play — Loss of hole; Stroke play — Two strokes.*

Rule 33-1g.

HAZARDS

Player T's ball lies in the water hazard in front of green. He may drop a ball, under penalty of one stroke, either:

a. Behind the water hazard, keeping the spot (C) at which the ball last crossed the margin of the water hazard between himself and the hole, and with no limit to how far behind the water hazard the ball may be dropped (the line of dropping is X - X - X - X);

or

b. As near as possible to the spot from which the original ball was played; if the stroke was played from the teeing ground, the ball may be teed anywhere within the teeing ground. **Rule 33-2.**

▫ MARGIN OF WATER HAZARD
• MARGIN OF LATERAL WATER HAZARD

Thus, brook between A-A and B-B is lateral water hazard; other parts of brook are regular water hazard. C and D — spots where balls last crossed hazard margin.

Player Q's ball has entered the lateral water hazard at left. He may, under penalty of one stroke, either:

a. Drop a ball behind the lateral water hazard, keeping the spot (D) at which the ball last crossed the margin of the lateral water hazard between himself and the hole (the line of dropping is Z - Z - Z - Z);

or

b. Drop a ball as near as possible to the spot from which the original ball was played; if the stroke was played from the teeing ground, the ball may be teed anywhere within the teeing ground;

or

c. Drop a ball outside the hazard within two club-lengths of the point (D) where the ball last crossed the hazard margin or a point on the opposite margin of the hazard equidistant from the hole. The ball must be dropped and come to rest not nearer the hole than point D. Thus, Player Q may drop a ball on either area marked E. **Rule 33-3.**

PENALTY FOR BREACH OF RULE: *Match play — Loss of hole; *Stroke play — Two strokes.*

*NOTE: In stroke play, in the event of a serious breach of Rule 33, see Rules 21-3c and 21-3d.

[62]

DOUBT WHETHER BALL IN WATER HAZARD

"If my ball is lost in the water hazard, I can save distance."

It is a question of fact whether a ball lost after having been struck toward a water hazard is lost inside or outside the hazard. In order to treat the ball as lost in the hazard, there must be reasonable evidence that the ball lodged therein. In the absence of such evidence, the ball must be treated as a lost ball and Rule 29-1 applies. **Rule 33-3, Note 2.**

THE FLAGSTICK

ATTENDED, REMOVED, OR HELD UP

Before and during the stroke, the player may have the flagstick attended, removed or held up to indicate the position of the hole. This may be done only on the authority of the player before he plays his stroke. If the flagstick be attended or removed by an opponent, a fellow-competitor or the caddie of either with the knowledge of the player and no objection is made, the player shall be deemed to have authorized it.

Rule 34-1.

PENALTY FOR BREACH OF RULE: *Match play — Loss of hole; Stroke play — Two strokes.*

THE FLAGSTICK

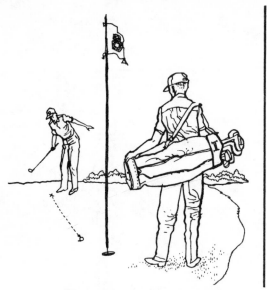

If a player or a caddie attend or remove the flagstick or stand near the hole while a stroke is being played, he shall be deemed to attend the flagstick until the ball comes to rest.

If the flagstick be not attended before the stroke is played, it shall not be attended or removed while the ball is in motion. **Rule 34-1**.

PENALTY FOR BREACH OF RULE: *Match play — Loss of hole; Stroke play — Two strokes.*

BALL RESTING AGAINST FLAGSTICK

If the ball rest against the flagstick when it is in the hole, the player shall be entitled to have the flagstick removed, and if the ball fall into the hole the player shall be deemed to have holed out at his last stroke; otherwise the ball, if moved, shall be placed on the lip of the hole, without penalty.

Rule 34-4.

A ball is "holed" when it lies within the circumference of the hole and all of it is below the level of the lip of the hole. **Definition 4**.

BALL STRIKING FLAGSTICK OR ATTENDANT

*Flagstick Unattended
Play Off Green*

*Flagstick Unattended
Play From Green*

*Flagstick Attended
Play From or Off Green*

The player's ball shall not strike either: —

a. The flagstick when attended or removed by the player, his partner, or either of their caddies, or by another person with the knowledge or authority of the player; or

b. The player's caddie, his partner or his partner's caddie when attending the flagstick, or another person attending the flagstick with the knowledge or authority of the player, or equipment carried by any such person; or

c. The flagstick in the hole, unattended, when the ball has been played from the putting green.

Rule 34-3.

PENALTY FOR BREACH OF RULE: *Match play — Loss of hole; Stroke play — Two strokes, and the ball shall be played as it lies.*

THE PUTTING GREEN

a. Touching Line of Putt.

The line of the putt must not be touched except as provided in Clauses 1b, 1c and 1d of Rule 35, or in measuring (Rule 20-1), or in removing movable obstructions (Rule 31-1), but the player may place the club in front of the ball in addressing it without pressing anything down.

b. Loose Impediments.

The player may move sand, loose soil, or any loose impediment on the putting green by picking them up or brushing them aside with his hand or a club without pressing anything down. If the ball be moved, it shall be replaced, without penalty.

c. Repair of Hole Plugs and Ball Marks.

The player or his partner may repair an old hole plug or damage to the putting green caused by the impact of a ball. If the player's ball lie on the putting green, it may be lifted to permit repair and shall be replaced on the spot from which it was lifted; in match play the ball must be replaced immediately if the opponent so requests.

If a ball be moved during such repair, it shall be replaced without penalty.

d. Lifting and Cleaning Ball.

A ball lying on the putting green may be lifted, without penalty, cleaned if desired and replaced on the spot from which it was lifted; in match play the ball must be replaced immediately if the opponent so requests. **Rule 35-1d.**

Spike marks on the line of putt. They may not be pressed down or otherwise repaired.

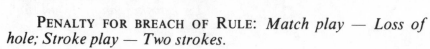

PENALTY FOR BREACH OF RULE: *Match play — Loss of hole; Stroke play — Two strokes.*

DIRECTION FOR PUTTING

"Putt it for here."

Club touching green

WRONG

Club held off green

RIGHT

WRONG

When the player's ball is on the putting green, the player's caddie, his partner or his partner's caddie may, before the stroke is played, point out a line for putting, but the line of the putt shall not be touched in front of, to the side of, or behind the hole.

While making the stroke, the player shall not allow his caddie, his partner or his partner's caddie to position himself on or close to an extension of the line of putt behind the ball.

No mark shall be placed anywhere on the putting green to indicate a line for putting. **Rule 35-1e.**

PENALTY FOR BREACH OF RULE: *Match play — Loss of hole; Stroke play — Two strokes.*

BALL TO BE MARKED WHEN LIFTED

Before a ball on the putting green is to be lifted, its position shall be marked. If the player fail so to mark the position of the ball, the player shall incur a penalty of one stroke and the ball shall be replaced. NOTE: The position of a lifted ball should be marked by placing a ball-marker, or other small object on the putting green, immediately behind the ball; if the marker interfere with the play, stance or stroke of another player, it should be placed one or more putterhead-lengths to one side. **Rule 35-1k.**

PENALTY FOR BREACH OF RULE: *Match play — Loss of hole; Stroke play — Two strokes.*

THE PUTTING GREEN

BALL IN MOTION—OTHER BALL TO BE AT REST

While the player's ball is in motion after a stroke on the putting green, an opponent's or a fellow-competitor's ball shall not be played or touched. **Rule 35-1g.**

PENALTY FOR BREACH OF RULE: *Match play—Loss of hole; Stroke play — Two strokes.*

BALL OVERHANGING HOLE

"I suppose I have to play now."

When any part of the ball overhangs the edge of the hole, the owner of the ball is not allowed more than a few seconds to determine whether it is at rest. If by then the ball has not fallen into the hole, it is deemed to be at rest.

Rule 35-1i.

PENALTY FOR BREACH OF RULE: *Match play — Loss of hole; Stroke play — Two strokes.*

BALL ON A WRONG PUTTING GREEN

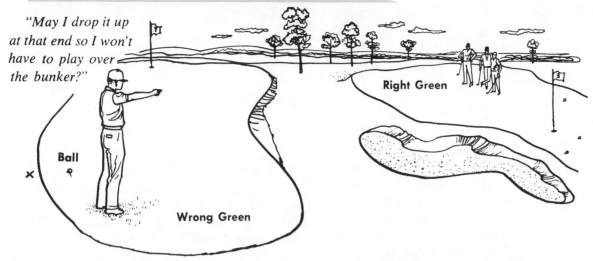

"May I drop it up at that end so I won't have to play over the bunker?"

Ball

Wrong Green

Right Green

The player must drop off the green within one club-length of point X.

If a ball lie on a putting green other than that of the hole being played, the nearest point shall be determined which (a) is not nearer the hole and (b) is not in a hazard or on a putting green. The player shall lift the ball and drop it without penalty within one club-length of the point thus determined on ground which fulfils (a) and (b) above.

STANDING ASTRIDE OR ON LINE OF PUTT

The player shall not make a stroke on the putting green from a stance astride, or with either foot touching, the line of the putt or an extension of that line behind the ball. For the purpose of Rule 35-1L only, the line of putt does not extend beyond the hole. **Rule 35-1L.**

PENALTY FOR BREACH OF RULE: *Match play — Loss of hole; Stroke play — Two strokes.*

THE PUTTING GREEN

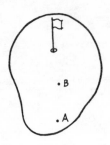

MATCH PLAY

A alone can determine whether B's ball shall be lifted while A plays. When the player's ball lies on the putting green, if the player consider that the opponent's ball interfere with his play, he may require that the opponent's ball be lifted. The opponent's ball shall be replaced after the player has played his stroke. If the player's ball stop on the spot formerly occupied by the lifted ball, the player shall first play another stroke before the lifted ball is replaced. If a ball be accidentally moved in complying with this Rule, no penalty shall be incurred and the ball shall be replaced. **Rule 35-2a.**

PENALTY FOR BREACH OF RULE: *Loss of hole.*

STROKE PLAY

Interference

If A thinks B's ball may interfere with A's play, A can require B's ball to be lifted or played, at B's option. When the competitor's ball lies on the putting green, if the competitor consider that the fellow-competitor's ball interfere with his play, he may require that the fellow-competitor's ball be lifted or played, at the fellow-competitor's option.

If a ball be accidentally moved in complying with this Rule, no penalty shall be incurred and the ball shall be replaced.

NOTE: It is recommended that the interfering ball be played, rather than lifted, unless the subsequent play of a fellow-competitor is likely to be affected. **Rule 35-3a.**

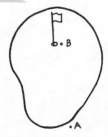

Match Play

If B thinks his ball may assist A, B has no authority to lift it. A is entitled to such assistance. If B had lifted his ball, A could require him to replace it (Rule 35-1d).

Stroke Play

If B thinks his ball may assist A, B may lift or play first.

If the fellow-competitor consider that his ball lying on the putting green might be of assistance to the competitor, the fellow-competitor may lift or play first. **Rule 35-3b.**

BALL MOVING ANOTHER BALL

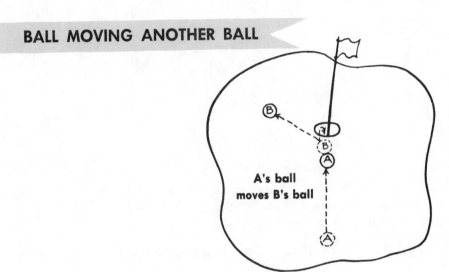

A's ball
moves B's ball

MATCH PLAY

If A's ball knocks B's ball into the hole, B has holed out at his last stroke.

If A's ball moves B's ball otherwise, B may replace his ball or leave it where it came to rest, at his option, but this must be done before another stroke is played by either side. If A's ball stop on the spot formerly occupied by B's ball, and B declare his intention to replace his ball, A shall first play another stroke, after which B shall replace his ball.

Rule 35-2c.

PENALTY FOR BREACH OF RULE: *Loss of hole.*

(Three-Ball, Best-Ball and Four-Ball match play — Rule 40-1c.)

STROKE PLAY

When both balls lie on the putting green, if the competitor's ball strike a fellow-competitor's ball, the competitor shall incur a penalty of two strokes and shall play his ball as it lies. The fellow-competitor's ball shall be at once replaced. **Rule 35-3c.**

THE PUTTING GREEN

PLAYING OUT OF TURN — MATCH PLAY

If a player play when his opponent should have done so, the opponent may immediately require the player to replay the stroke, in which case the player shall replace his ball and play in correct order, without penalty. **Rule 35-2b**.

PENALTY FOR BREACH OF RULE: *Loss of hole.*

CONCEDING OPPONENT'S NEXT STROKE — MATCH PLAY

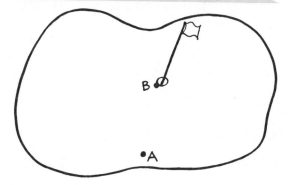

When the opponent's ball has come to rest, the player may concede the opponent to have holed out with his next stroke and may remove the opponent's ball with a club or otherwise. If the player does not concede the opponent's next stroke and the opponent's ball fall into the hole, the opponent shall be deemed to have holed out with his last stroke. If the opponent's next stroke has not been conceded, the opponent shall play without delay in correct order. **Rule 35-2d**.

PENALTY FOR BREACH OF RULE: *Loss of hole.*

COMBINING MATCH AND STROKE PLAY PROHIBITED

"Can't we kill two birds with one stone today — play our match in the club championship and also compete in the weekly medal play?"

"No — it wouldn't be right."

Certain special rules governing stroke play are so substantially different from those governing match play that combining the two forms of play is not practicable and is not permitted. The results of matches played and the scores returned in these circumstances shall not be accepted. **Rule 36-1.**

COURSE UNPLAYABLE

If the Committee or its authorized representative consider that for any reason the course is not in a playable condition, or that there are circumstances which render the proper playing of the game impossible, it shall have the power in match and stroke play to order a temporary suspension of play, or in stroke play to declare play null and void and to cancel all scores for the round in question.

When a round is cancelled, all penalties incurred in that round are cancelled.

When play has been temporarily suspended, it shall be resumed from where it was discontinued, even though resumption occur on a subsequent day. **Rule 36-4c.**

(Procedure in discontinuing play — Rule 37-6b.)

THE COMMITTEE

DEFINING BOUNDS AND MARGINS

"Am I in a water hazard or not?"

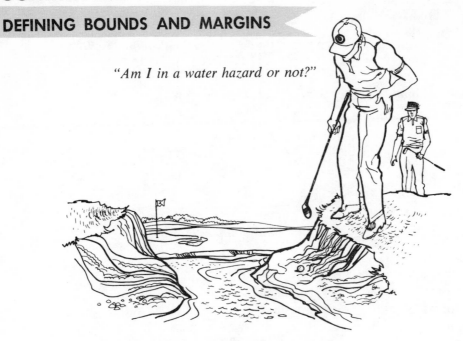

The Committee shall define accurately:

a. The course and out of bounds.
b. The margins of water hazards and lateral water hazards.
c. Ground under repair.
d. Obstructions. **Rule 36-6**.

LOCAL RULE WAIVING PENALTY PROHIBITED

"There's a Local Rule here — no penalty for dropping out of a water hazard. That's wrong."

A penalty imposed by a Rule of Golf shall not be waived by a Local Rule. **Rule 36-7b**.

KNOWING CONDITIONS OF PLAY

The player shall be responsible for acquainting himself with the conditions under which the competition is to be played. **Rule 37-1.**

BREACH OF RULE BY CADDIE

"Those last fellows certainly scuffed up the green."

"You can't do that!"

For any breach of a Rule or a Local Rule by his caddie, the player incurs the relative penalty. **Rule 37-2.**

Rule 35-1a provides that the line of the putt must not be touched (with exceptions which do not apply here), under penalty of loss of hole in match play or two strokes in stroke play.

THE PLAYER

CHECKING HANDICAP

Before starting in a handicap competition, the player shall ensure that his current handicap is recorded correctly on the official list, if any, for the competition and on the card issued for him by the Committee. In the case of match play or bogey, par or Stableford competitions, he shall inform himself of the holes at which strokes are given or taken.

If a player play off a higher handicap than his current one, *he shall be disqualified* from the handicap competition. If he play off a lower one, the score, or the result of the match, shall stand. **Rule 37-4.**

DISCONTINUANCE OF PLAY

The player shall not discontinue play on account of bad weather or for any other reason, unless:

He considers that there be danger from lightning,

or

There be some other reason, such as sudden illness, which the Committee considers satisfactory.

If the player discontinue play without specific permission from the Committee, he shall report to the Committee as soon as possible.

General Exception: Players discontinuing match play by agreement are not subject to disqualification unless by so doing the competition is delayed. **Rule 37-6a.**

PENALTY FOR BREACH OF RULE: *Disqualification.*

UNDUE DELAY

The player shall at all times play without undue delay. Between the completion of a hole and driving off the next tee, the player may not delay in any way. **Rule 37-7.**

PENALTY FOR BREACH OF RULE: *Match play — Loss of hole; Stroke play — Two strokes. For repeated offense — Disqualification.*

If the player delay play between holes, he is delaying the play of the next hole, and the penalty applies to that hole.

ARTIFICIAL DEVICES

Except as provided for under the Rules, the player shall not use any artificial device:
   a. Which might assist him in making a stroke or in his play;
   b. For the purpose of gauging or measuring distance or conditions which affect his play; or
   c. Which, not being part of the grip (see Appendix IId), is designed to give him artificial aid in gripping the club. **Rule 37-9**. (Exceptions to Rule 37-9c: Plain gloves and material or substance applied to the grip such as tape, gauze or resin.).

PENALTY FOR BREACH OF RULE: *Disqualification.*

SCORING IN STROKE PLAY

CHECKING SCORES IN STROKE PLAY

Stroke Play: The competitor shall check his score for each hole, settle any doubtful points with the Committee, ensure that the marker has signed the card, countersign the card himself, and return it to the Committee as soon as possible. The competitor is solely responsible for the correctness of the score recorded for each hole.

PENALTY FOR BREACH OF RULE: *Disqualification.*

The Committee is responsible for the addition of scores and application of the handicap recorded on the card. **Rule 38-2**.

Exception: Four-ball stroke play — Rule 41-1d.

NO ALTERATION OF SCORES IN STROKE PLAY

"May I see that card I turned in about an hour ago? I think I put down a 5 for the 18th, but I actually had a 6."

Stroke Play: No alteration may be made on a card after the competitor has returned it to the Committee.

If the competitor return a score for any hole lower than actually taken, *he shall be disqualified.*

A score higher than actually taken must stand as returned.
Rule 38-3.

Exception: Four-ball stroke play — Rule 41-8a.

THREE-BALL, BEST-BALL AND FOUR-BALL PLAY

For definitions of these forms of play, see page 18.

BALL INFLUENCING PLAY

Bill

"Jim, please mark your ball. As it is, it could help our opponents."

Jim →

Match Play

Any player may have any ball (except the ball about to be played) lifted if he consider that it might interfere with or be of assistance to a player or side, but this may not be done while any ball in the match is in motion. **Rule 40-1b.**

Four-Ball Stroke Play

Any competitor may have any ball (except the ball about to be played) lifted or played, at the option of the owner, if he consider that it might be of assistance to a competitor or side, but this may not be done while any ball in the group is in motion.

If the owner of the ball refuse to comply with the above when required to do so, his side shall be disqualified. **Rule 41-2.**

ORDER OF PLAY

"You putt first, partner, so I can get some idea about the line."

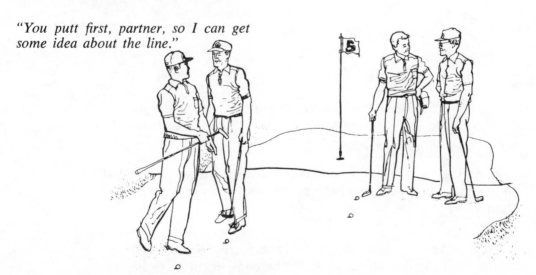

Match Play and Stroke Play

Balls belonging to the same side may be played in the order the side considers best. **Rules 40-3a, 41-5.**

THREE-BALL, BEST-BALL AND FOUR-BALL PLAY

PLAYING OUT OF TURN

Bill

"You played out of turn, partner. Bill was away."

Match Play

On the teeing ground, if a player play when an opponent should have played, the opponent may immediately require the player to abandon the ball so played and to play a ball in correct order.

Through the green or in a hazard, a player shall incur no penalty if he play when an opponent should have done so. The stroke shall not be replayed.

On the putting green, if a player play when an opponent should have done so, the opponent may immediately require the player to replay the stroke in correct order, without penalty. **Rule 40-1d.**

Stroke Play

If a competitor play out of turn, no penalty shall be incurred. The ball shall be played as it lies. **Rules 41-1a, 20-3.**

BALL STRUCK BY ANOTHER BALL

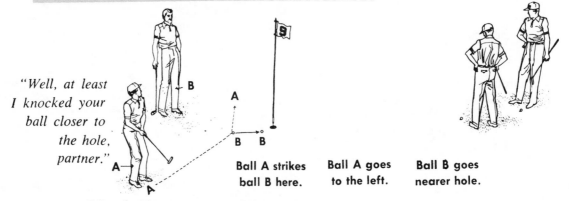

"Well, at least I knocked your ball closer to the hole, partner."

Ball A strikes ball B here.   Ball A goes to the left.   Ball B goes nearer hole.

Match Play

There is no penalty if a player's ball move any other ball in the match. The owner of the moved ball shall replace it. **Rule 40-1c.**

Stroke Play

When the balls concerned lie on the putting green, if a competitor's ball strike any other ball, the competitor shall incur a penalty of two strokes and shall play his ball as it lies. The other ball shall be at once replaced.

In all other cases, if a competitor's ball strike any other ball, the competitor shall play his ball as it lies. The owner of the moved ball shall replace his ball, without penalty. **Rule 41-4.**

THREE-BALL, BEST-BALL AND FOUR-BALL PLAY

BALL STOPPED OR DEFLECTED

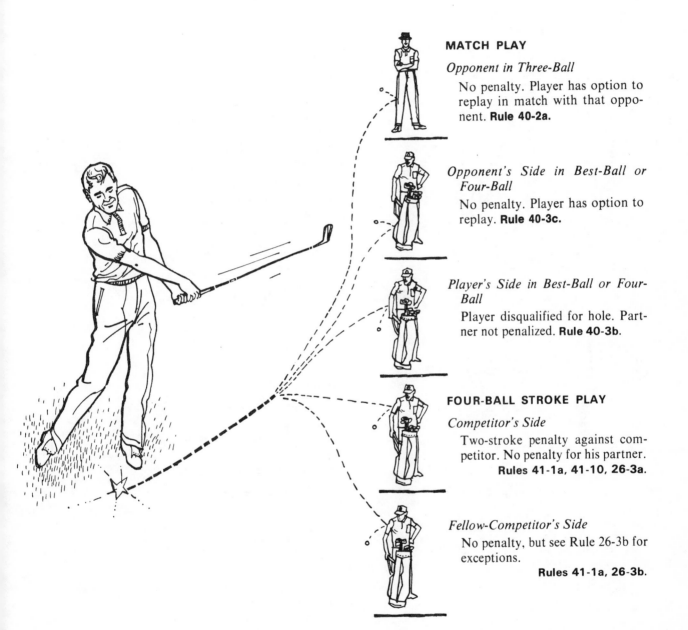

MATCH PLAY

Opponent in Three-Ball

No penalty. Player has option to replay in match with that opponent. **Rule 40-2a.**

Opponent's Side in Best-Ball or Four-Ball

No penalty. Player has option to replay. **Rule 40-3c.**

Player's Side in Best-Ball or Four-Ball

Player disqualified for hole. Partner not penalized. **Rule 40-3b.**

FOUR-BALL STROKE PLAY

Competitor's Side

Two-stroke penalty against competitor. No penalty for his partner. **Rules 41-1a, 41-10, 26-3a.**

Fellow-Competitor's Side

No penalty, but see Rule 26-3b for exceptions. **Rules 41-1a, 26-3b.**

THREE-BALL, BEST-BALL AND FOUR-BALL PLAY

MATCH PLAY

By Opponent in Three-Ball

Opponent is penalized one stroke in match with owner of ball, but not in match with other opponent. Ball is replaced. **Rule 40-2b.**

By Player's Side Accidentally in Best-Ball or Four-Ball

Owner of ball is penalized one stroke. Partner not penalized. Ball is replaced. **Rule 40-3e.**

By Opponent's Side in Best-Ball or Four-Ball

Opponent responsible is penalized one stroke. Other opponent is not penalized. Ball is replaced.

Rule 40-3f.

FOUR-BALL STROKE PLAY

By Competitor's Side Accidentally

One-stroke penalty against competitor. No penalty for his partner. Ball is replaced.

Rules 41-1a, 41-10, 27-1d.

By Fellow-Competitor's Side

No penalty, but see Rule 27-3 for exception. Ball is replaced.

Rules 41-1a, 41-10, 27-3.

The following suggestions are offered for learning how to apply the Rules of Golf to specific cases:

1. Become familiar with key words and special terms in the language of the Rules; thus, FLAGSTICK, not pin; BUNKER, not trap; STROKE PLAY, not medal play; LATERAL WATER HAZARD, not parallel water hazard.

2. Study the Definitions carefully. They are basic. Note, for instance, such differences as "loose impediments" for certain *natural* objects (Definition 17) and "obstructions" for *artificial* objects (Definition 20). The Rules do not mention "fairway" or "rough"; both are covered by "through the green" (Definition 35).

3. What form of play is involved? Is it match play or stroke play? Single or four-ball? A four-ball match is *not* a foursome (Definition 28). Example: When one ball on the putting green interferes with another in a single match only the player away may require the interfering ball to be lifted (Rules 35-2a); but in a four-ball match *any* player may have the ball removed (Rule 40-lb).

4. Where did the incident occur? — on the teeing ground, "through the green," in a hazard, or on the putting green? Find the right place in the Index, as the Rules may be different for the same occurences on different parts of the course.

5. Two Rules may cover different aspects of the same case. Rule 27-1a calls for a ball moved by an outside agency to be replaced but it does not provide the solution if the spot is not determinable. The solution is provided by Rule 22-3c.

6. Every word means what it says.

7. Carry a Rules book in your golf bag and use it whenever an incident arises.

8. Committees will find helpful information in the USGA Appendix.

THE RULES OF GOLF

Section I
ETIQUETTE

Courtesy on the Course

Consideration for Other Players
In the interest of all, players should play without delay.
No player should play until the players in front are out of range.
Players searching for a ball should signal the players behind them to pass as soon as it becomes apparent that the ball will not easily be found: they should not search for five minutes before doing so. They should not continue play until the players following them have passed and are out of range.
When the play of a hole has been completed, players should immediately leave the putting green.

Behavior During Play
No one should move, talk or stand close to or directly behind the ball or the hole when a player is addressing the ball or making a stroke.
The player who has the honor should be allowed to play before his opponent or fellow-competitor tees his ball.

Priority on the Course

In the absence of special rules, two-ball matches should have precedence of and be entitled to pass any three- or four-ball match.
A single player has no standing and should give way to a match of any kind.
Any match playing a whole round is entitled to pass a match playing a shorter round.
If a match fails to keep its place on the course and loses more than one clear hole on the players in front, it should allow the match following to pass.

Care of the Course

Holes in Bunkers
Before leaving a bunker, a player should carefully fill up and smooth over all holes and footprints made by him.

Restore Divots, Repair Ball-Marks and Damage by Spikes
Through the green, a player should ensure that any turf cut or displaced by him is replaced at once and pressed down, and that any damage to the putting green made by the ball is carefully repaired. Damage to the putting green caused by golf shoe spikes should be repaired *on completion of the hole.*

Damage to Greens—Flagsticks, Bags, etc.
Players should insure that, when putting down bags, or the flagstick, no damage is done to the putting green, and that neither they nor their caddies damage the hole by standing close to it, in handling the flagstick or in removing the ball from the hole. The flagstick should be properly replaced in the hole before the players leave the putting green. Players should not damage the putting green by leaning on their putters, particularly when removing the ball from the hole.

Golf Carts
Local Notices regulating the movement of golf carts should be strictly observed.

Damage Through Practice Swings
In taking practice swings, players should avoid causing damage to the course, particularly the tees, by removing divots.

Section II
DEFINITIONS

1. Addressing the Ball
A player has "addressed the ball" when he has taken his stance (Definition 29) and has also grounded his club, except that in a hazard a player has addressed the ball when he has taken his stance.

2. Advice
"Advice" is any counsel or suggestion which could influence a player in determining his play, the choice of a club, or the method of making a stroke.
Information on the Rules or Local Rules is not advice.

3. Ball Deemed to Move
A ball is deemed to have "moved" if it leave its position and come to rest in any other place.

4. Ball Holed
A ball is "holed" when it lies within the circumference of the hole and all of it is below the level of the lip of the hole.

5. Ball in Play, Provisional Ball, Wrong Ball
a. A ball is "in play" as soon as the player has made a stroke on

the teeing ground. It remains as his ball in play until holed out, except when it is out of bounds, lost or lifted, or another ball has been substituted under an applicable Rule or Local Rule: a ball so substituted becomes the ball in play.

b. A "provisional ball" is a ball played under Rule 30 for a ball which may be lost outside a water hazard or may be out of bounds. It ceases to be a provisional ball when the Rule provides *either* that the player continue play with it as the ball in play *or* that it be abandoned.

c. A "wrong ball" is any ball other than the ball in play or a provisional ball or, in stroke play, a second ball played under Rule 11-5 or under Rule 21-3d.

6. Ball Lost
A ball is "lost" if:

a. It be not found, or be not identified as his by the player, within five minutes after the player's side or his or their caddies have begun to search for it; *or*

b. The player has put another ball into play under the Rules, even though he may not have searched for the original ball; *or*

c. The player has played any stroke with a provisional ball from a point nearer the hole than the place where the original ball is likely to be, whereupon the provisional ball becomes the ball in play.

Time spent in playing a wrong ball is not counted in the five minute period allowed for search.

7. Caddie, Forecaddie and Equipment
a. A "caddie" is one who carries or handles a player's clubs during play and otherwise assists him in accordance with the Rules.

When one caddie is employed by more than one player, he is always deemed to be the caddie of the player whose ball is involved, and equipment carried by him is deemed to be that player's equipment, except when the caddie acts upon specific directions of another player, in which case he is considered to be that other player's caddie.

Note: *In threesome, foursome, best-ball and four-ball play, a caddie carrying for more than one player should be assigned to the members of one side.*

b. A "forecaddie" is one employed by the Committee to indicate to players the position of balls on the course, and is an outside agency (Definition 22).

c. "Equipment" is anything used, worn or carried by or for the player except his ball in play. Equipment includes a golf cart. If such a cart is shared by more than one player, its status under the Rules is the same as that of a caddie employed by more than one player.

8. Casual Water
"Casual water" is any temporary accumulation of water which is visible before or after the player takes his stance and is not in a water hazard. Snow and ice are either casual water or loose impediments, at the option of the player.

9. Committee
The "Committee" is the committee in charge of the competition or, if the matter does not arise in a competition, the committee in charge of the course.

10. Competitor
A "competitor" is a player in a stroke competition. A "fellow-competitor" is any person with whom the competitor plays. Neither is partner of the other.

In stroke play foursome and four-ball competitions, where the context so admits, the word "competitor" or "fellow-competitor" shall be held to include his partner.

11. Course
The "course" is the whole area within which play is permitted. It is the duty of the Committee to define its boundaries accurately.

12. Flagstick
The "flagstick" is a movable straight indicator provided by the Committee, with or without bunting or other material attached, centered in the hole to show its position. It shall be circular in cross-section.

13. Ground Under Repair
"Ground under repair" is any portion of the course so marked by order of the Committee or so declared by its authorized representative. It includes material piled for removal and a hole made by a greenkeeper, even if not so marked. Stakes and lines defining ground under repair are in such ground.

Note: *Grass cuttings and other material left on the course which have been abandoned and are not intended to be removed are not ground under repair unless so marked.*

14. Hazards
A "hazard" is any bunker, water hazard or lateral water hazard. Bare patches, scrapes, roads, tracks and paths are not hazards.

It is the duty of the Committee to define accurately the extent of the water hazards. That part of a water hazard to be played as a lateral water hazard should be distinctively marked. Stakes and lines defining the margins of hazards are in the hazards.

a. A "bunker" is an area of bare ground, often a depression, which is usually covered with sand. Grass-covered ground bordering or within a bunker is *not* part of the hazard.

b. A "water hazard" is any sea, lake, pond, river, ditch, surface drainage ditch or other open water course (regardless of whether or not it contains water), and anything of a similar nature. All ground or water within the margin of a water hazard, whether or not it be covered with any growing substance, is part of the water hazard. The margin of a water hazard is deemed to extend vertically upwards.

c. A "lateral water hazard" is a water hazard or that part of a water hazard so situated that it is not possible or is deemed by the Committee to be impracticable to drop a ball behind the water hazard and keep the spot at which the ball last crossed the margin of the hazard between the player and the hole.

Note: *Water hazards should be defined by yellow stakes or lines and lateral water hazards by red stakes or lines.*

15. Hole
The "hole" shall be 4¼ inches in diameter and at least 4 inches deep. If a lining be used, it shall be sunk at least 1 inch below the putting green surface unless the nature of the soil makes it impractical to do so; its outer diameter shall not exceed 4¼ inches.

16. Honor
The side which is entitled to play first from the teeing ground is said to have the "honor."

17. Loose Impediments
The term "loose impediments" denotes natural objects not fixed or growing and not adhering to the ball, and includes stones not solidly embedded, leaves, twigs, branches and the like, dung, worms and insects and casts or heaps made by them.

Snow and ice are either casual water or loose impediments, at the option of the player.

Sand and loose soil are loose impediments on the putting green, but not elsewhere on the course.

18. Marker
A "marker" is a scorer in stroke play who is appointed by the Committee to record a competitor's score. He may be a fellow-competitor. He is not a referee.

A marker should not lift a ball or mark its position unless authorized to do so by the competitor and, unless he is a fellow-competitor, should not attend the flagstick or stand at the hole or mark its position.

19. Observer
An "observer" is appointed by the Committee to assist a referee to decide questions of fact and to report to him any breach of a Rule or Local Rule. An observer should not attend the flagstick, stand at or mark the position of the hole, or lift the ball or mark its position.

20. Obstructions
An "obstruction" is anything artificial, whether erected, placed or left on the course, including the artificial surfaces and sides of roads and paths but excepting:—

a. Objects defining out of bounds, such as walls, fences, stakes and railings;

b. In water hazards, artificially surfaced banks or beds, including bridge supports when part of such a bank. Bridges and bridge supports which are not part of such a bank are obstructions;

c. Any construction declared by the Committee to be an integral part of the course.

21. Out of Bounds
"Out of bounds" is ground on which play is prohibited.

When out of bounds is fixed by stakes or a fence, the out of bounds line is determined by the nearest inside points of the stakes or fence posts at ground level; the line is deemed to extend vertically upwards. When out of bounds is fixed by a line on the ground, the line itself is out of bounds.

A ball is out of bounds when all of it lies out of bounds.

22. Outside Agency
An "outside agency" is any agency not part of the match or, in stroke play, not part of a competitor's side, and includes a referee, a marker, an observer, or a forecaddie employed by the Committee. Neither wind nor water is an outside agency.

23. Partner

A "partner" is a player associated with another player on the same side.

In a threesome, foursome or a four-ball where the context so admits, the word "player" shall be held to include his partner.

24. Penalty Stroke

A "penalty stroke" is one added to the score of a side under certain Rules. It does not affect the order of play.

25. Putting Green

The "putting green" is all ground of the hole being played which is specially prepared for putting or otherwise defined as such by the Committee.

A ball is deemed to be on the putting green when any part of it touches the putting green.

26. Referee

A "referee" is a person who has been appointed by the Committee to accompany players to decide questions of fact and of golf law. He shall act on any breach of Rule or Local Rule which he may observe or which may be reported to him by an observer (Definition 19).

In stroke play the Committee may limit a referee's duties.

A referee should not attend the flagstick, stand at or mark the position of the hole, or lift the ball or mark its position.

27. Rub of the Green

A "rub of the green" occurs when a ball in motion is accidentally stopped or deflected by any outside agency.

28. Sides and Matches

SIDE: A player, or two or more players who are partners.

SINGLE: A match in which one plays against another.

THREESOME: A match in which one plays against two, and each side plays one ball.

FOURSOME: A match in which two play against two, and each side plays one ball.

THREE-BALL: A match in which three play against one another, each playing his own ball.

BEST-BALL: A match in which one plays against the better ball of two or the best ball of three players.

FOUR-BALL: A match in which two play their better ball against the better ball of two other players.

Note: *In a best-ball or four-ball match, if a partner be absent for reasons satisfactory to the Committee, the remaining member(s) of his side may represent the side.*

29. Stance

Taking the "stance" consists in a player placing his feet in position for and preparatory to making a stroke.

30. Stipulated Round

The "stipulated round" consists of playing the holes of the course in their correct sequence unless otherwise authorized by the Committee. The number of holes in a stipulated round is 18 unless a smaller number is authorized by the Committee.

In match play only, the Committee may, for the purpose of settling a tie, extend the stipulated round to as many holes as are required for a match to be won.

31. Stroke

A "stroke" is the forward movement of the club made with the intention of fairly striking at and moving the ball.

32. Teeing

In "teeing," the ball may be placed on the ground, on an irregularity of surface created by the player on the ground or on sand or other substance in order to raise it off the ground.

33. Teeing Ground

The "teeing ground" is the starting place for the hole to be played. It is a rectangular area two club-lengths in depth, the front and the sides of which are defined by the outside limits of two tee-markers. A ball is outside the teeing ground when all of it lies outside the stipulated area.

When playing the first stroke with any ball (including a provisional ball) from the teeing ground, the tee-markers are immovable obstructions (Definition 20).

34. Terms Used in Reckoning in Match Play

In match play, the reckoning of holes is kept by the terms:—so many "holes up" or "all square," and so many "to play."

A side is "dormie" when it is as many holes up as there are holes remaining to be played.

35. Through the Green

"Through the green" is the whole area of the course except:—
a. Teeing ground and putting green of the hole being played;
b. All hazards on the course.

36. Types of Club

There are three recognized types of golf club:—

An "iron" club is one with a head which usually is relatively narrow from face to back, and usually is made of steel.

A "wood" club is one with a head relatively broad from face to back, and usually is made of wood, plastic or a light metal.

A "putter" is a club designed primarily for use on the putting green — see Definition 25.

Section III
THE RULES OF PLAY

Rule 1
The Game

The Game of Golf consists in playing a ball from the teeing ground into the hole by successive strokes in accordance with the Rules.

PENALTY FOR BREACH OF RULE:
Match play—Loss of hole; Stroke play—Disqualification.

Rule 2
The Club (Def. 36) and the Ball

The United States Golf Association and the Royal and Ancient Golf Club of St. Andrews reserve the right to change the Rules and the interpretations regulating clubs and balls at any time.

1. Legal Clubs and Balls

The player's clubs, and the balls he uses, shall conform with Clauses 2 and 3 of this Rule.

2. Form and Make of Clubs

a. GENERAL CHARACTERISTICS

The golf club shall be composed of a shaft and a head, and all of the various parts shall be fixed so that the club is one unit; the club shall not be designed to be adjustable, except for weight.

Note: *Playing characteristics not to be changed during a round—Rule 2-2b.*

The club shall not be substantially different from the traditional and customary form and make, and shall conform with the regulations governing the design of clubs at Appendix II and the specifications for markings on clubs at Appendix III.

b. PLAYING CHARACTERISTICS NOT TO BE CHANGED

The playing characteristics of a club shall not be purposely changed during a round; foreign material shall not be added to the club face at any time.

Note: *Players in doubt as to the legality of clubs are advised to consult the USGA. If a manufacturer is in doubt as to the legality of a club which he proposes to manufacture, he should submit a sample to the USGA for a ruling, such sample to become the property of the USGA for reference purposes.*

3. The Ball

a. SPECIFICATIONS

The weight of the ball shall be *not greater* than 1.620 ounces avoirdupois, and the size *not less* than 1.680 inches in diameter.

The velocity of the ball shall be not greater than 250 feet per second when measured on apparatus approved by the USGA: a maximum tolerance of 2% will be allowed. The temperature of the ball when so tested shall be 75 degrees Fahrenheit.

A brand of golf ball, when tested on apparatus approved by the USGA on the outdoor range at the USGA Headquarters under the conditions set forth in the Overall Distance Standard for golf balls on file with the USGA, shall not cover an average distance in carry and roll exceeding 280 yards, plus a tolerance of 8%. (Note: The 8% tolerance will be reduced to a minimum of 4% as test techniques are improved.)

Exception:— In international team competitions, the size of the ball shall be *not less* than 1.620 inches in diameter and the Overall Distance Standard shall not apply.

Note: *The Rules of the Royal and Ancient Golf Club of St. Andrews, Scotland, provide that the weight of the ball shall be not greater than 1.620 ounces avoirdupois, the size not less than 1.620 inches in diameter and the velocity not greater than 250 feet per second (with 2% tolerance) when measured on apparatus approved by the Royal and Ancient Golf Club.*

b. FOREIGN MATERIAL PROHIBITED

Foreign material shall not be applied to a ball for the purpose of changing its playing characteristics.

PENALTY FOR BREACH OF RULE: *Disqualification.*

Rule 3
Maximum of Fourteen Clubs

1. Selection and Replacement of Clubs

The player shall start a stipulated round with not more than fourteen clubs. He is limited to the clubs thus selected for that round except that, without unduly delaying play, he may:—

a. If he started with fewer than fourteen, add as many as will bring his total to that number;

b. Replace, with any club, a club which becomes unfit for play in the normal course of play.

The addition or replacement of a club or clubs may not be made by borrowing from any other person playing on the course.

2. Side May Share Clubs

Partners may share clubs provided that the total number of clubs carried by the side does not exceed fourteen.

PENALTY FOR BREACH OF RULE 3-1 OR 3-2, REGARDLESS OF NUMBER OF WRONG CLUBS CARRIED:

Match play—Loss of one hole for each hole at which any violation occurred; maximum penalty per round: loss of two holes. The penalty shall be applied to the state of the match at the conclusion of the hole at which the violation is discovered, provided all players in the match have not left the putting green of the last hole of the match.

Bogey and Par Competitions—Penalties as in Match play.

Stroke play—Two strokes for each hole at which any violation occurred; maximum penalty per round: four strokes.

Stableford Competitions—From total points scored for the round, deduction of two points for each hole at which any violation occurred; maximum deduction per round: four points.

Note: *A serious breach of this Rule should be dealt with by the Committee under Rule 1.*

3. Wrong Club Declared Out of Play

Any club carried or used in violation of this Rule shall be declared out of play by the player immediately upon discovery and thereafter shall not be used by the player during the round under *penalty of disqualification.*

Rule 4
Agreement to Waive Rules Prohibited

Players shall not agree to exclude the operation of any Rule or Local Rule or to waive any penalty incurred.

PENALTY FOR BREACH OF RULE:

Match play—Disqualification of both sides;
Stroke play—Disqualification of competitors concerned.

Rule 5
General Penalty

Except when otherwise provided for, the penalty for a breach of a Rule or Local Rule is:

Match play—Loss of hole;
Stroke play—Two strokes.

Rule 6
Match Play

1. Winner of Hole

In match play the game is played by holes.

Except as otherwise provided for in the Rules, a hole is won by the side which holes its ball in the fewer strokes. In a handicap match the lower net score wins the hole.

2. Halved Hole

A hole is halved if each side holes out in the same number of strokes.

When a player has holed out and his opponent has been left with a stroke for the half, nothing that the player who has holed out can do shall deprive him of the half which he has already gained; but if the player thereafter incur any penalty, the hole is halved.

3. Winner of Match

A match (which consists of a stipulated round, unless otherwise decreed by the Committee) is won by the side which is leading by a number of holes greater than the number of holes remaining to be played.

Rule 7
Stroke Play

1. Winner

The competitor who holes the stipulated round or rounds in the fewest strokes is the winner.

2. Failure to Hole Out

If a competitor fail to hole out at any hole before he has played a stroke from the next teeing ground, or, in the case of the last hole of the round, before he has left the putting green, *he shall be disqualified. (Ball purposely moved, touched or lifted—Rules 27-1c and 35-1k.)*

Rule 8
Practice

1. During Play of Hole

During the play of a hole, a player shall not play any practice stroke.

PENALTY FOR BREACH OF RULE 8-1:

Match play—Loss of hole; Stroke play—Two strokes.

2. Between Holes

Between the play of two holes, a player shall not play a practice stroke from any hazard, or on or to a putting green other than that of the hole last played.

PENALTY FOR BREACH OF RULE 8-2:

*Match play—Loss of hole; Stroke play—Two strokes.
*The penalty applies to the next hole.

3. Stroke Play

On any day of a stroke competition or play-off, a competitor shall not practice on the competition course before a round or play-off. When a competition extends over consecutive days, practice on the competition course between rounds is prohibited.

If a competition extending over consecutive days is to be played on more than one course, practice between rounds on any competition course remaining to be played is prohibited.

Note: *The Committee may, at its discretion, waive or modify these prohibitions in the conditions of the competition (Appendix 1-12).*

PENALTY FOR BREACH OF RULE 8-3: *Disqualification.*
(Duty of Committee to define practice ground—Rule 36-4b.)

Note 1: *A practice swing is not a practice stroke and may be taken at any place on the course provided the player does not violate the Rules.*

Note 2: *Unless otherwise decided by the Committee, there is no penalty for practice on the course on any day of a match play competition.*

Rule 9
Advice (Def. 2) and Assistance

1. Giving or Asking for Advice; Receiving Assistance

a. ADVICE

A player may give advice to, or ask for advice from, only his partner or either of their caddies.

b. ASSISTANCE

In making a stroke, a player shall not seek or accept physical assistance or protection from the elements.

2. Indicating Line of Play

Except on the putting green, a player may have the line of play indicated to him by anyone, but no one shall stand on or close to the line while the stroke is being played. Any mark placed during the play of a hole by the player or with his knowledge to indicate the line shall be removed before the stroke is played.

(Indicating line of play on putting green—Rule 35-1e.)
PENALTY FOR BREACH OF RULE:
Match play—Loss of hole; Stroke play—Two strokes.

Rule 10
Information as to Strokes Taken

1. General
The number of strokes a player has taken shall include any penalty strokes incurred.

2. Match Play
A player who has incurred a penalty shall inform his opponent as soon as possible. If he fail to do so, he shall be deemed to have given wrong information.

An opponent is entitled to ascertain from the player, during the play of a hole, the number of strokes he has taken and, after play of a hole, the number of strokes taken on the hole just completed.

If during the play of a hole the player give or be deemed to give wrong information as to the number of strokes taken, he shall incur no penalty if he correct the mistake before his opponent has played his next stroke. If after play of a hole the player give or be deemed to give wrong information as to the number of strokes taken on the hole just completed, he shall incur no penalty if he correct his mistake before any player plays from the next teeing ground or, in the case of the last hole of the match, before all players leave the putting green. If the player fail so to correct the wrong information, *he shall lose the hole.*

3. Stroke Play
A competitor who has incurred a penalty should inform his marker as soon as possible.

Rule 11
Disputes, Decisions and Doubt as to Rights

1. Claims and Penalties
a. MATCH PLAY
In match play, if a dispute or doubt arise between the players on any point, in order that a claim may be considered it must be made before any player in the match plays from the next teeing ground or, in the case of the last hole of the match, before all players in the match leave the putting green. No later claim shall be considered unless it is based on facts previously unknown to the player making the claim and the player making the claim had been given wrong information (Rule 10) by an opponent. In any case, however, no later claim shall be considered after the result of the match has been officially announced, unless the Committee is satisfied that the opponent knew he was giving wrong information.
b. STROKE PLAY
In stroke play, no penalty shall be imposed after the competition is closed unless the Committee is satisfied that the competitor has knowingly returned a score for any hole lower than actually taken (Rule 38-3); no penalty shall be rescinded after the competition is closed. A competition is deemed to have closed:—
In stroke play only—When the result of the competition is officially announced.
In stroke play qualifying followed by match play—When the player has teed off in his first match.

2. Referee's Decision
If a referee has been appointed by the Committee, his decision shall be final.

3. Committee's Decision
In the absence of a referee, the players shall refer any dispute to the Committee, whose decision shall be final.

If the Committee cannot come to a decision, it shall refer the dispute to the USGA Rules of Golf Committee whose decision shall be final.

If the point in dispute or doubt has not been referred to the Rules of Golf Committee, the player or players have the right to refer an agreed statement through the Secretary of the Club to the Rules of Golf Committee for an opinion as to the correctness of the decision given. The reply will be sent to the Secretary of the Club or Clubs concerned.

If play be conducted other than in accordance with the Rules of Golf, the Rules of Golf Committee will not give a decision on any question.

4. Decision by Equity
If any point in dispute be not covered by the Rules or Local Rules, the decision shall be made in accordance with equity.

5. Stroke Play: Doubt as to Procedure
In stroke play only, when during play of a hole a competitor is doubtful of his rights or procedure, he may, without penalty, play a second ball. After the doubtful situation has arisen and before taking further action, he should announce to his marker his decision to proceed under this Rule and which ball he will score with if the Rules permit.

On completing the round, the competitor must report the facts immediately to the Committee; if he fail to do so, *he shall be disqualified.* If the Rules allow the procedure selected in advance by the competitor, the score with the ball selected shall be his score for the hole. Should the competitor fail to announce in advance his procedure or selection, the ball with the higher score shall count if the Rules allow the procedure adopted for such ball.

Note 1: *A second ball played under Rule 11-5 is not a provisional ball under Rule 30.*
Note 2: *The privilege of playing a second ball does not exist in match play.*

Rule 12
The Honor (Def. 16)

1. The Honor
a. MATCH PLAY
A match begins by each side playing a ball from the first teeing ground in the order of the draw. In the absence of a draw, the option of taking the honor shall be decided by lot.
The side which wins a hole shall take the honor at the next teeing ground. If a hole has been halved, the side which had the honor at the previous teeing ground shall retain it.
b. STROKE PLAY
The honor shall be taken as in match play.

2. Playing out of Turn
a. MATCH PLAY
If, on the teeing ground, a player play when his opponent should have played, the opponent may immediately require the player to abandon the ball so played and to play a ball in correct order, without penalty.
b. STROKE PLAY
If, on the teeing ground, a competitor by mistake play out of turn, no penalty shall be incurred and the ball shall be in play.
c. SECOND BALL FROM TEE
If a player play a second ball, including a provisional ball, from the tee, he should do so after the opponent or the fellow-competitor has played his first stroke. If a player play a second ball out of turn, the provisions of Clauses 2a and 2b of this Rule apply.

Rule 13
Playing Outside Teeing Ground (Def. 33)

1. Match Play
If a player, when starting a hole, play a ball from outside the teeing ground, the opponent may immediately require the player to replay the stroke, in which case the player shall tee a ball and play the stroke from within the teeing ground, without penalty.

2. Stroke Play
If a competitor, when starting a hole, play from outside the teeing ground, *he shall be penalized two strokes* and shall then play from within the teeing ground. Strokes played by a competitor from outside the teeing ground do not count in his score. If the competitor fail to rectify his mistake before making a stroke on the next teeing ground or, in the case of the last hole of the round, before leaving the putting green, *he shall be disqualified.*

Note: STANCE. *A player may take his stance outside the teeing ground to play a ball within it.*

Rule 14
Ball Falling Off Tee

If a ball, when not in play, fall off a tee or be knocked off a tee by the player in addressing it, it may be re-teed without penalty, but if a stroke be made at the ball in these circumstances, whether the ball be moving or not, the stroke shall be counted but no penalty shall be incurred.

Rule 15
Order of Play in Threesome or Foursome

1. General

In a threesome or a foursome, the partners shall strike off alternately from the teeing grounds, and thereafter shall strike alternately during the play of each hole. Penalty strokes (Definition 24) do not affect the order of play.

2. Match Play

If a player play when his partner should have played, *his side shall lose the hole.* In a match comprising more than one stipulated round, the partners shall not change the order of striking from the teeing grounds after any stipulated round.

3. Stroke Play

If the partners play a stroke or strokes in incorrect order, such stroke or strokes shall be cancelled, and *the side shall be penalized two strokes.* A ball shall then be put in play as nearly as possible at the spot from which the side first played in incorrect order. This must be done before a stroke has been played from the next teeing ground, or, in the case of the last hole of the round, before the side has left the putting green. If they fail to do so, *they shall be disqualified.* If the first ball was played from the teeing ground, a ball may be teed anywhere within the teeing ground; if from through the green or a hazard, it shall be dropped; if on the putting green, it shall be placed.

Note: *As in stroke play a stipulated round cannot be more than 18 holes (Def. 30), the order of play between partners may be changed for a second or subsequent round, unless the conditions of the competition provide otherwise.*

Rule 16
Ball Played as It Lies; Embedded Ball

1. General

The ball shall be played as it lies, except as otherwise provided for in the Rules or Local Rules.

(Ball at Rest Moved by Player, Purposely—Rule 27-1c.)
(Ball at Rest Moved by Player, Accidentally—Rule 27-1d.)
(Ball at Rest Moving Accidentally after Address—Rule 27-1f.)

2. Embedded Ball

A ball embedded in its own pitch-mark in any closely mown area through the green may be lifted and dropped, without penalty, as near as possible to the spot where it lay but not nearer the hole.

PENALTY FOR BREACH OF RULE 16-2:
Match play—Loss of hole; Stroke Play—Two strokes.

Rule 17
Improving Lie or Stance and Influencing Ball Prohibited

1. Improving Line of Play or Lie Prohibited

A player shall not improve, or allow to be improved, his line of play, the position or lie of his ball or the area of his intended swing by moving, bending or breaking anything fixed or growing, or by removing or pressing down sand, loose soil, cut turf placed in position or other irregularities of surface except:—

a. As may occur in the course of fairly taking his stance;

b. In making the stroke or the backward movement of his club for the stroke;

c. On the teeing ground a player may create or eliminate irregularities of surface;

d. In repairing damage to the putting green under Rule 35-1c.

The club may be grounded only lightly and must not be pressed on the ground.

(Sand and loose soil on the putting green—Def. 17 and Rule 35-1b.)

(Removal of obstructions—Rule 31-1.)

Note: *Things fixed include objects defining out of bounds.*

2. Long Grass and Bushes

If a ball lie in long grass, rushes, bushes, whins, heather or the like, only so much thereof shall be touched as will enable the player to find and identify his ball; nothing shall be done which may in any way improve its lie.

The player is not of necessity entitled to see the ball when playing a stroke.

3. Building of Stance Prohibited

A player is always entitled to place his feet firmly on the ground when taking his stance, but he is not allowed to build a stance.

4. Exerting Influence on Ball

No player or caddie shall take any action to influence the position or the movement of a ball except in accordance with the Rules.

PENALTY FOR BREACH OF RULE:
Match play—Loss of hole; Stroke play—Two strokes.

Note: *In the case of a serious breach of Rule 17-4, the Committee may impose a penalty of disqualification.*

Rule 18
Loose Impediments (Def. 17)

Any loose impediment may be removed without penalty except when both the impediment and the ball lie in or touch a hazard. When a player's ball is in motion, a loose impediment on his line of play shall not be removed.

PENALTY FOR BREACH OF RULE:
Match play—Loss of hole; Stroke play—Two strokes.
(Ball moving after loose impediment touched—Rules 27-1e and 35-1b.)
(Finding ball in hazard—Rule 33-1e.)

Rule 19
Striking at Ball

1. Ball to be Fairly Struck at

The ball shall be fairly struck at with the head of the club and must not be pushed, scraped or spooned.

PENALTY FOR BREACH OF RULE 19-1:
Match play—Loss of hole; Stroke play—Two strokes.

2. Striking Ball Twice

If a player strike the ball twice when making a stroke, he shall count the stroke and *add a penalty stroke,* making two strokes in all.

(Playing a moving ball—Rule 25.)

Rule 20
Ball Farther from the Hole Played First

1. General

When the balls are in play, the ball farther from the hole shall be played first. If the balls are equidistant from the hole, the option of playing first should be decided by lot.

A player or a competitor incurs no penalty if a ball is moved in measuring to determine which ball is farther from the hole. A ball so moved shall be replaced.

2. Match Play

Through the green or in a hazard, if a player play when his opponent should have done so, the opponent may immediately require the player to replay the stroke. In such a case, the player shall drop a ball as near as possible to the spot from which his previous stroke was played, and play in correct order without penalty.

Exception: Three-ball, best-ball and four-ball match play. See Rule 40-1d.

PENALTY FOR BREACH OF RULE 20-2: *Loss of hole.*
(Playing out of turn on putting green—Rule 35-2b.)

3. Stroke Play

If a competitor play out of turn, no penalty shall be incurred. The ball shall be played as it lies.

Rule 21
Playing a Wrong Ball (Def. 5) or from a Wrong Place

1. General

A player must hole out with the ball driven from the teeing ground unless a Rule or Local Rule permit him to substitute another ball.

2. Match Play

a. WRONG BALL

If a player play a stroke with a wrong ball (Def. 5) except in a hazard, *he shall lose the hole.*

If a player play any strokes in a hazard with a wrong ball, there is no penalty provided he then play the correct ball; the strokes so played with a wrong ball do not count in the player's score.

If the wrong ball belong to another player, its owner shall place a ball on the spot from which the wrong ball was played.

When the player and the opponent exchange balls during the play of a hole, the first to play the wrong ball other than from a hazard shall lose the hole; when this cannot be determined, the hole shall be played out with the balls exchanged.

b. BALL PLAYED FROM WRONG PLACE

If a player play a stroke with a ball which has been dropped or placed under an applicable Rule but in a wrong place, *he shall lose the hole.*

Note: *For a ball played outside teeing ground, see Rule 13-1.*

3. Stroke Play

a. WRONG BALL

If a competitor play a stroke with a wrong ball (Def. 5) except in a hazard, *he shall add two penalty strokes to his score* and shall then play the correct ball.

If a competitor play any strokes in a hazard with a wrong ball, there is no penalty provided he then play the correct ball.

Strokes played with a wrong ball do not count in a competitor's score.

If the wrong ball belong to another player, its owner shall place a ball on the spot from which the wrong ball was played.

b. RECTIFICATION AFTER HOLING OUT

If a competitor hole out with a wrong ball, he may rectify his mistake by proceeding in accordance with Clause 3a of this Rule, subject to the prescribed penalty, provided he has not made a stroke on the next teeing ground, or, in the case of the last hole of the round, has not left the putting green. *The competitor shall be disqualified* if he does not so rectify his mistake.

c. BALL PLAYED FROM WRONG PLACE

If a competitor play a stroke with a ball which has been dropped or placed under an applicable Rule but in a wrong place, *he shall add two penalty strokes to his score* and play out the hole with that ball. If a serious breach of the applicable Rule is involved, *the competitor shall be disqualified* unless the breach has been rectified as provided by Rule 21-3d.

Note: *For a ball played outside the teeing ground, see Rule 13-2.*

d. RECTIFICATION

If a serious breach of the applicable Rule under Rule 21-3c may be involved and the competitor has not made a stroke on the next teeing ground or, in the case of the last hole of the round, has not left the putting green, the competitor may rectify any such serious breach by *adding two penalty strokes to his score*, dropping or placing a ball in accordance with the applicable Rule and playing out the hole. On completion of the round, the competitor must report the facts immediately to the Committee, which shall determine whether a serious breach of the Rule was involved and, accordingly, whether the score with the ball played under this Rule 21-3d shall count.

Note: *Penalty strokes incurred by playing the ball ruled not to count and strokes subsequently taken with that ball shall be disregarded.*

Rule 22
Lifting, Dropping and Placing

1. Lifting

A ball to be lifted under the Rules or Local Rules may be lifted by the player, his partner or another person authorized by the player. In any such case, the player shall be responsible for any breach of the Rules or Local Rules.

Note: *A referee or observer should not lift a ball or mark its position (Defs. 19 and 26).*

2. Dropping

a. HOW TO DROP

A ball to be dropped under the Rules or Local Rules shall be dropped by the player himself. He shall face the hole, stand erect, and drop the ball behind him over his shoulder. If a ball be dropped in any other manner and remain the ball in play (Definition 5), *the player shall incur a penalty stroke.*

If the ball touch the player before it strikes the ground, the player shall re-drop without penalty. If the ball touch the player after it strikes the ground, or if it come to rest against the player and move when he then moves, there is no penalty, and the ball shall be played as it lies.

b. WHERE TO DROP

When a ball is to be dropped, it shall be dropped as near as possible to the spot where the ball lay, but not nearer the hole, except when a Rule permits it to be dropped elsewhere or placed. In a hazard, the ball must come to rest in that hazard; if it roll out of the hazard, it must be re-dropped, without penalty.

c. WHEN TO RE-DROP

If a dropped ball roll into a hazard, onto a putting green, out of bounds or more than two club-lengths from the point where it first struck the ground, or come to rest nearer the hole than its original position, it shall be re-dropped, without penalty. If the ball again roll into such a position, it shall be placed where it first struck the ground when re-dropped.

PENALTY FOR BREACH OF RULE 22-2:
Match play—Loss of hole; Stroke play—Two strokes.

3. Placing

a. HOW AND WHERE TO PLACE

A ball to be placed under the Rules or Local Rules shall be placed by the player or his partner. A ball to be replaced shall be replaced by the player, his partner or the person who lifted it, on the spot where the ball lay. In any such case, the player shall be responsible for any breach of the Rules or Local Rules.

b. LIE OF BALL TO BE PLACED OR REPLACED ALTERED

If the original lie of a ball to be placed or replaced has been altered, the ball shall be placed in the nearest lie most similar to that which it originally occupied, not more than two club-lengths from the original lie and not nearer the hole.

c. SPOT NOT DETERMINABLE

If it be impossible to determine the spot where the ball is to be placed, through the green or in a hazard, the ball shall be dropped, or on the putting green it shall be placed, as near as possible to the place where it lay but not nearer the hole.

d. BALL MOVING

If a ball when placed fail to remain on the spot on which it was placed, it shall be replaced without penalty. If it still fail to remain on that spot, it shall be placed at the nearest spot not nearer the hole where it can be placed at rest.

PENALTY FOR BREACH OF RULE 22-3:
Match play—Loss of hole; Stroke play—Two strokes.

4. Ball in Play when Dropped or Placed

A ball dropped or placed under a Rule governing the particular case is in play (Definition 5) and shall not be lifted or re-dropped or replaced except as provided in the Rules.

5. Lifting Ball Wrongly Dropped or Placed

A ball dropped or placed but not played may be lifted without penalty if:—

a. It was dropped or placed under a Rule governing the particular case but not in the right place or otherwise not in accordance with that Rule. The player shall then drop or place the ball in accordance with the governing Rule.

b. It was dropped or placed under a Rule which does not govern the particular case. The player shall then proceed under a Rule which governs the case. However, in match play, if, before the opponent plays his next stroke, the player fail to inform him that the ball has been lifted, *the player shall lose the hole.*

Note: *In stroke play, in the event of a serious breach of Rule 22, see Rules 21-3c and 21-3d.*

Rule 23
Identifying or Cleaning Ball

The responsibility for playing the proper ball rests with the player. Each player should put an identification mark on his ball.

1. Identifying Ball

Except in a hazard, the player may, without penalty, lift his ball in play for the purpose of identification and replace it on the spot from which it was lifted, provided this is done in the presence of his opponent in match play or his marker in stroke play. If the player lift his ball for identification in a hazard, or elsewhere other than in the presence of his opponent or marker, *he shall incur a penalty of one stroke*, and the ball shall be replaced.

(Touching grass, etc. for identification—Rule 17-2.)

2. Cleaning Ball

A ball may be cleaned when lifted as follows:—

From an embedded lie under Rule 16-2;
From an unplayable lie under Rule 29-2;
For relief from an obstruction under Rule 31;
From casual water, ground under repair or otherwise under Rule 32;
From a water hazard under Rule 33-2 or 33-3;
On the putting green under Rule 35-1d or on a wrong putting green under Rule 35-1j;
For identification under Rule 23-1, but the ball may be cleaned only to the extent necessary for identification; or

Under a Local Rule permitting cleaning the ball.

If the player clean his ball during the play of a hole except as permitted under this Rule, *he shall incur a penalty of one stroke*, and the ball if lifted shall be replaced.

Note: *If a player who is required to replace a ball fail to do so, the general penalty for breach of Rule 22-3a will apply in addition to any other penalty incurred.*

Rule 24
Ball Interfering with Play

When the player's ball lies through the green or in a hazard, the player may have any other ball lifted if he consider that it interfere with his play. A ball so lifted shall be replaced after the player has played his stroke.

If a ball be accidentally moved in complying with this Rule, no penalty shall be incurred and the ball shall be replaced.

(Lie of ball to be placed or replaced altered—Rule 22-3b.)
(Putting green—Rule 35-2a and 35-3a.)
PENALTY FOR BREACH OF RULE:
Match play—Loss of hole; Stroke play—Two strokes.

Rule 25
A Moving Ball

1. Playing Moving Ball Prohibited

A player shall not play while his ball is moving.
Exceptions:—
Ball falling off tee—Rule 14.
Striking ball twice—Rule 19-2.
As hereunder—Rule 25-2.

When the ball only begins to move after the player has begun the stroke or the backward movement of his club for the stroke, he shall incur no penalty under this Rule, but he is not exempted from the provisions for:—

Ball at Rest Moved by Player, Accidentally—Rule 27-1d.

Ball at Rest Moving after Loose Impediment Touched—Rule 27-1e.

Ball at Rest Moving Accidentally after Address—Rule 27-1f.

2. Ball Moving in Water

When a ball is in water in a water hazard, the player may, without penalty, make a stroke at it while it is moving, but he must not delay to make his stroke in order to allow the wind or current to better the position of the ball. A ball moving in water in a water hazard may be lifted if the player elect to invoke Rule 33-2 or 33-3.

PENALTY FOR BREACH OF RULE:
Match play—Loss of hole; Stroke play—Two strokes.

Rule 26
Ball in Motion Stopped or Deflected

1. General

a. BY OUTSIDE AGENCY

If a ball in motion be accidentally stopped or deflected by any outside agency, it is a rub of the green and the ball shall be played as it lies, without penalty.

b. LODGING IN OUTSIDE AGENCY

If a ball lodge in any moving or animate outside agency, the player shall, through the green or in a hazard, drop a ball, or on the putting green place a ball, as near as possible to the spot where the object was when the ball lodged in it, without penalty.

Exception to Rule 26-1: On putting green—Rule 35-1h.

2. Match Play

a. BY PLAYER

If a player's ball be stopped or deflected by himself, his partner or either of their caddies or equipment, *he shall lose the hole.*

b. BY OPPONENT, ACCIDENTALLY

If a player's ball be accidentally stopped or deflected by an opponent, his caddie or equipment, no penalty shall be incurred. The player may play the ball as it lies or, before another stroke is played by either side, he may cancel the stroke, place a ball on the spot where the ball previously lay and replay the stroke.

Exception:—Ball striking person attending flagstick—Rule 34-3b.

(Ball purposely stopped or deflected by opponent—Rule 17-4.)
(Ball striking opponent's ball—Rule 27-2b.)

3. Stroke Play

a. BY COMPETITOR

If a competitor's ball be stopped or deflected by himself, his

partner or either of their caddies or equipment, *the competitor shall incur a penalty of two strokes.* The ball shall be played as it lies, except when it lodges in the competitor's, his partner's or either of their caddies' clothes or equipment, in which case the competitor shall, through the green or in a hazard, drop the ball, or on the putting green place the ball, as near as possible to where the article was when the ball lodged in it.

b. BY FELLOW-COMPETITOR

If a competitor's ball be accidentally stopped or deflected by a fellow-competitor, his caddie, ball or equipment, it is a rub of the green and the ball shall be played as it lies.

Exceptions:—

Ball lodging in fellow-competitor's clothes, etc.—Clause 1b of this Rule.

On the putting green, ball striking fellow-competitor's ball in play—Rule 35-3c.

Ball played from putting green stopped or deflected by fellow-competitor or his caddie—Rule 35-1h.

Ball striking person attending flagstick—Rule 34-3b.

PENALTY FOR BREACH OF RULE:
Match play—Loss of hole; Stroke play—Two strokes.

Note: *If the referee or the Committee determine that a ball has been deliberately stopped or deflected by an outside agency, including a fellow-competitor or his caddie, further procedure should be prescribed in equity under Rule 11-4. On the putting green, Rule 35-1h applies.*

Rule 27
Ball at Rest Moved (Def. 3)

1. General

a. BY OUTSIDE AGENCY

If a ball at rest be moved by any outside agency, the player shall incur no penalty and shall replace the ball before playing another stroke.

(Opponent's ball moved by player's ball—Rule 27-2b.)

Note 1: *Neither wind nor water is an outside agency.*

Note 2: *If the ball moved is not immediately recoverable, another ball may be substituted.*

b. DURING SEARCH

During search for a ball, if it be moved by an opponent, a fellow-competitor or the equipment or caddie of either, no penalty shall be incurred. The player shall replace the ball before playing another stroke.

c. BY PLAYER, PURPOSELY

When a ball is in play, if a player, his partner or either of their caddies purposely move, touch or lift it, except as provided for in the Rules or Local Rules, *the player shall incur a penalty stroke* and the ball shall be replaced. The player may, however, without penalty, touch the ball with his club in the act of addressing it, provided the ball does not move (Def. 3).

(On putting green—Rule 35-1k.)

d. BY PLAYER, ACCIDENTALLY

When a ball is in play, if a player, his partner, their equipment or either of their caddies accidentally move it, or by touching anything cause it to move, except as provided for in the Rules or Local Rules, *the player shall incur a penalty stroke.* The ball shall be replaced unless the movement of the ball occurs after the player has begun his swing and he does not discontinue his swing.

(Ball accidentally moved when measuring to determine which ball farther from the hole—Rule 20-1.)

(Ball accidentally moved in the process of marking—Rule 35-2a or 35-3a.)

e. BALL MOVING AFTER LOOSE IMPEDIMENT TOUCHED

Through the green, if the ball move before the player has addressed it but after any loose impediment lying within a club-length of it has been touched by the player, his partner or either of their caddies, the player shall be deemed to have caused the ball to move. *The penalty shall be one stroke.* The ball shall be replaced unless the movement of the ball occurs after the player has begun his swing and he does not discontinue his swing.

(Loose impediment on putting green—Rule 35-1b.)

f. BALL MOVING ACCIDENTALLY AFTER ADDRESS

If a ball in play move after the player has addressed it (Def. 1), he shall be deemed to have caused it to move and *shall incur a penalty stroke*, and the ball shall be played as it lies.

2. Match Play

a. BY OPPONENT

If a player's ball be touched or moved by an opponent, his caddie or equipment (except as otherwise provided in the Rules), *the opponent shall incur a penalty stroke.* The player shall replace the ball before playing another stroke.

b. OPPONENT'S BALL MOVED BY PLAYER'S BALL

If a player's ball move an opponent's ball, no penalty shall be incurred. The opponent may either play his ball as it lies or, before another stroke is played by either side, he may replace the ball.

If the player's ball stop on the spot formerly occupied by the opponent's ball and the opponent declare his intention to replace the ball, the player shall first play another stroke, after which the opponent shall replace his ball.

(Putting green—Rule 35-2c.)
(Three-Ball, Best-Ball and Four-Ball match play—Rule 40-1c.)

3. Stroke Play
BALL MOVED BY A FELLOW-COMPETITOR

If a competitor's ball be moved by a fellow-competitor, his caddie, ball or equipment, no penalty shall be incurred. The competitor shall replace his ball before playing another stroke.

*Exception to penalty:—*Ball striking fellow-competitor's ball on putting green—Rule 35-3c.

PENALTY FOR BREACH OF RULE:
*Match play—Loss of hole; *Stroke play—Two strokes*
(Playing a wrong ball—Rule 21.)

Note 1: *If a player who is required to replace a ball fail to do so, the general penalty for a breach of this Rule will apply in addition to any other penalty incurred.*

Note 2: *If it be impossible to determine the spot on which a ball is to be placed or if a ball when placed fail to remain on the spot on which it was placed, Rule 22-3 applies.*

*Note 3: *In stroke play, in the event of a serious breach of Rule 27, see Rules 21-3c and 21-3d.*

Rule 28
Ball Unfit for Play

The ball may be deemed unfit for play when it is visibly cut or out of shape or so cracked, pierced or otherwise damaged as to interfere with its true flight or true roll or its normal behavior when struck. The ball shall not be deemed unfit for play solely because mud or other material adhere to it, its surface be scratched or its paint be damaged or discolored.

If a player has reason to believe his ball is unfit for play, the player, after he has announced his intention to proceed under this Rule to his opponent in match play or marker in stroke play, may, without penalty, lift his ball in play for the purpose of determining whether it is unfit. If the ball is so damaged as to be unfit for play, the player may substitute another ball, placing it on the spot where the original ball lay. Substitution may only be made on the hole during the play of which the damage occurred.

If a ball break into pieces as a result of a stroke, a ball shall be placed where the original ball lay and the stroke shall be replayed, without penalty.

A player is not the sole judge as to whether his ball is unfit for play. If the opponent or the marker dispute a claim of unfitness, the referee, if one is present, or the Committee shall settle the matter (Rule 11-2 or 11-3).

PENALTY FOR BREACH OF RULE:
Match play—Loss of hole; Stroke play—Two strokes.
(Ball unplayable—Rule 29-2.)

Rule 29
Ball Lost (Def. 6),
Out of Bounds (Def. 21),
or Unplayable

1. Lost or Out of Bounds
a. PROCEDURE

If a ball be lost outside a water hazard or be out of bounds, the player shall play his next stroke as nearly as possible at the spot from which the original ball was played or moved by him, *adding a penalty stroke* to his score for the hole. If the original stroke was played from the teeing ground, a ball may be teed anywhere within the teeing ground; if from through the green or a hazard, it shall be dropped; if on the putting green, it shall be placed.

(Ball lost in casual water, ground under repair, etc.—Rule 32-4.)
b. ASCERTAINING LOCATION

A player has the right at any time of ascertaining whether his opponent's ball is out of bounds.

A person outside the match may point out the location of a ball for which search is being made.

c. STANDING OUT OF BOUNDS

A player may stand out of bounds to play a ball lying within bounds.

2. Unplayable
a. PLAYER SOLE JUDGE

The player is the sole judge as to whether his ball is unplayable.

It may be declared unplayable at any place on the course except in a water hazard (Rule 33-2, -3).

b. PROCEDURE

If the player deem his ball to be unplayable, he shall either:—
(i) Play his next stroke as provided in Clause 1a of this Rule *(stroke-and-distance penalty),*
or
(ii) Drop a ball, *under penalty of one stroke,* either (a) within two club-lengths of the point where the ball lay, but not nearer the hole, or (b) behind the point where the ball lay, keeping that point between himself and the hole, with no limit to how far behind that point the ball may be dropped: if the ball lay in a bunker and the player elect to proceed under this Clause (ii), a ball must be dropped in the bunker.

(Ball in casual water, etc.—Rule 32.)
(Ball unfit for play—Rule 28.)
PENALTY FOR BREACH OF RULE:
*Match play—Loss of hole; *Stroke play—Two strokes.*
*Note: *In stroke play, in the event of a serious breach of Rule 29, see Rules 21-3c and 21-3d.*

Rule 30
Provisional Ball (Def. 5)

1. Procedure
If a ball may be lost outside a water hazard or may be out of bounds, to save time the player may play another ball provisionally as nearly as possible from the spot at which the original ball was played. If the original ball was played from the teeing ground, the provisional ball may be teed anywhere within the teeing ground; if from through the green or a hazard, it shall be dropped; if on the putting green, it shall be placed.

a. The player must inform his opponent or marker that he intends to play a provisional ball, and he must play it before he or his partner goes forward to search for the original ball. If he fail to do so, and play another ball, such ball is not a provisional ball and becomes the ball in play *under penalty of stroke and distance* (Rule 29-1); the original ball is deemed to be lost (Def. 6b).

b. Play of a provisional ball from the teeing ground does not affect the order in which the sides play (Rule 12-2).

c. A provisional ball is never an outside agency.

2. Play of a Provisional Ball
a. The player may play a provisional ball until he reaches the place where the original ball is likely to be. If he play any strokes with the provisional ball from a point nearer the hole than that place, the original ball is deemed to be lost (Def. 6c).

b. If the original ball be lost outside a water hazard or be out of bounds, the provisional ball becomes the ball in play, *under penalty of stroke and distance* (Rule 29-1).

c. If the original ball be neither lost outside a water hazard nor out of bounds, the player shall abandon the provisional ball and continue play with the original ball. Should he fail to do so, any further strokes played with the provisional ball shall constitute playing a wrong ball and the provisions of Rule 21 shall apply.

PENALTY FOR BREACH OF RULE:
Match play—Loss of hole; Stroke play—Two strokes.

Note: *If the original ball be unplayable or lie or be lost in a water hazard, the player must proceed under Rule 29-2 or Rule 33-2 or 33-3, whichever is applicable.*

Rule 31
Obstructions (Def. 20)

1. Movable Obstruction May Be Removed
Any movable obstruction may be removed. If the ball be moved in so doing, it shall be replaced on the exact spot from which it was moved, without penalty. If it be impossible to determine the spot or to replace the ball, the player shall proceed in accordance with Rule 22-3.

When a ball is in motion, an obstruction on the player's line of play other than an attended flagstick and equipment of the players shall not be removed.

2. Interference by Immovable Obstruction
a. INTERFERENCE

Interference by an immovable obstruction occurs when the ball lies in or on the obstruction, or so close to the obstruction that the obstruction interferes with the player's stance or the area of his intended swing. The fact that an immovable obstruction intervenes on the line of play is not, of itself, interference under this Rule.

b. RELIEF

A player may obtain relief from interference by an immovable obstruction, without penalty, as follows:—

(i) *Through the Green:*

Through the green, the point nearest to where the ball lies shall be determined (without crossing over, through or under the obstruction) which (a) is not nearer the hole, (b) avoids interference as defined in Clause 2a of this Rule, and (c) is not in a hazard or on a putting green. He shall lift the ball and drop it within one club-length of the point thus determined on ground which fulfils (a), (b) and (c) above.

Note: *The prohibition against crossing over, through or under the obstruction does not apply to the artificial surfaces and sides of roads and paths or when the ball lies in or on the obstruction.*

(ii) *In a Hazard:*

In a hazard, the player may lift and drop the ball in accordance with Clause (i) above, except that the ball must be dropped in the hazard.

(iii) *On the Putting Green:*

On the putting green, the player may lift and place the ball in the nearest position to where it lay which affords relief from interference, but not nearer the hole.

c. RE-DROPPING

If a dropped ball roll into a position covered by this Rule, or nearer the hole than its original position, it shall be re-dropped without penalty. If it again roll into such a position, it shall be placed where it first struck the ground when re-dropped.

PENALTY FOR BREACH OF RULE:

Match play—Loss of hole; Stroke play—Two strokes.

Rule 32
Casual Water (Def. 8),
Ground Under Repair (Def. 13),
Hole Made by Burrowing Animal

1. Interference

Interference by casual water, ground under repair, or a hole, cast or runway made by a burrowing animal, a reptile or a bird occurs when a ball lies in or touches any of these conditions or when the condition interferes with the player's stance or the area of his intended swing. If interference exists, the player may either play the ball as it lies or take relief as provided in Clause 3 of this Rule.

2. Finding Ball

If a ball lying in casual water, ground under repair or a hole, cast or runway made by a burrowing animal, a reptile or a bird is not visible, the player may probe for it. If the ball be moved in such search, no penalty shall be incurred, and the ball shall be replaced unless the player elect to proceed under Clause 3 of this Rule.

3. Relief

If the player elect to take relief, he shall proceed as follows:—

a. *Through the Green*—Through the green, the point nearest to where the ball lies shall be determined which (a) is not nearer the hole, (b) avoids interference by the condition, and (c) is not in a hazard or on a putting green. The player shall lift the ball and drop it without penalty within one club-length of the point thus determined on ground which fulfils (a), (b) and (c) above.

b. *In a Hazard*—In a hazard, the player shall lift and drop the ball either:—

Without penalty, in the hazard as near as possible to the spot where the ball lay, but not nearer the hole, on ground which affords maximum relief from the condition;

or,

Under penalty of one stroke, outside the hazard, but not nearer the hole, keeping the spot where the ball lay between himself and the hole.

c. *On the Putting Green*—On the putting green, or if such condition on the putting green intervene between a ball lying on the putting green and the hole, the player shall lift the ball and place it without penalty in the nearest position to where it lay which affords maximum relief from the condition, but not nearer the hole nor in a hazard.

4. Ball Lost

a. *Outside a Hazard*—If a ball be lost under a condition covered by this Rule, except in a hazard, the player may take relief as follows: the point nearest to where the ball last crossed the margin of the area shall be determined which (a) is not nearer the hole than where the ball last crossed that margin, (b) avoids interference by the condition, and (c) is not in a hazard or on a putting green. He shall drop a ball without penalty within one club-length of the point thus determined on ground which fulfils (a), (b) and (c) above.

b. *In a Hazard*—If a ball be lost in a hazard under a condition covered by this Rule, the player may drop a ball either:—

Without penalty, in the hazard, but not nearer the hole than the spot at which the ball last crossed the margin of the area, on ground which affords maximum relief from the condition;

or,

Under penalty of one stroke, outside the hazard, but not nearer the hole, keeping the spot at which the ball last crossed the margin of the hazard between himself and the hole.

In order that a ball may be treated as lost under a condition covered by this Rule, there must be reasonable evidence to that effect.

5. Re-Dropping

If a dropped ball roll into the area from which relief was taken, or come to rest in such a position that that area still affects the player's stance or the area of his intended swing, the ball shall be re-dropped, without penalty. If the ball again roll into such a position, it shall be placed where it first struck the ground when re-dropped.

PENALTY FOR BREACH OF RULE:

Match play—Loss of hole; Stroke play—Two strokes.

Rule 33
Hazards (Def. 14)

1. Touching Hazard Prohibited

When a ball lies in or touches a hazard or a water hazard, nothing shall be done which may in any way improve its lie. Before making a stroke, the player shall not touch the ground in the hazard or water in the water hazard with a club or otherwise, nor touch or move a loose impediment lying in or touching the hazard, nor test the condition of the hazard or of any similar hazard; subject to the following considerations:—

a. STANCE

The player may place his feet firmly in taking his stance.

b. TOUCHING FIXED OR GROWING OBJECT

In addressing the ball or in the stroke or in the backward movement for the stroke, the club may touch any wooden or stone wall, paling or similar fixed object or any grass, bush, tree, or other growing substance (but the club may not be soled in the hazard).

c. OBSTRUCTIONS

The player is entitled to relief from obstructions under the provisions of Rule 31.

d. LOOSE IMPEDIMENT OUTSIDE HAZARD

Any loose impediment not in or touching the hazard may be removed.

e. FINDING BALL

If the ball be covered by sand, fallen leaves or the like, the player may remove as much thereof as will enable him to see the top of the ball. If the ball be moved in such removal, no penalty shall be incurred, and the ball shall be replaced.

If the ball is believed to be lying in water in a water hazard, the player may probe for it with a club or otherwise. If the ball be moved in such search, no penalty shall be incurred; the ball shall be replaced, unless the player elect to proceed under Clause 2 or 3 of this Rule.

The ball may not be lifted for identification.

f. PLACING CLUBS IN HAZARD

The player may, without penalty, place his clubs in the hazard prior to making a stroke, provided nothing is done which may improve the lie of the ball or constitute testing the soil.

g. SMOOTHING IRREGULARITIES

There is no penalty should soil or sand in the hazard be smoothed by the player after playing a stroke, or by his caddie at any time without the authority of the player, provided nothing is done that improves the lie of the ball or assists the player in his subsequent play of the hole.

h. CASUAL WATER, GROUND UNDER REPAIR

The player is entitled to relief from casual water, ground under repair, and otherwise as provided for in Rule 32.

i. INTERFERENCE BY A BALL

The player is entitled to relief from interference by another ball under the provisions of Rule 24.

2. Ball in Water Hazard (Def. 14b)

If a ball lie or be lost in a water hazard (whether the ball lie in water or not), the player may drop a ball *under penalty of one stroke*, either:—

a. Behind the water hazard, keeping the spot at which the ball last crossed the margin of the water hazard between himself and the hole, and with no limit to how far behind the water hazard the ball may be dropped,

or

b. As near as possible to the spot from which the original ball was played; if the stroke was played from the teeing ground, the ball may be teed anywhere within the teeing ground.

Note: *If a ball has been played from within a water hazard and has not crossed any margin of the hazard, the player may drop a ball behind the hazard under Rule 33-2a.*

3. Ball in Lateral Water Hazard (Def. 14c)

If a ball lie or be lost in a lateral water hazard, the player may, *under penalty of one stroke,* either:—

a. Play his next stroke in accordance with Clause 2a or 2b of this Rule,

or

b. Drop a ball outside the hazard within two club-lengths of (i) the point where the ball last crossed the margin of the hazard or (ii) a point on the opposite margin of the hazard equidistant from the hole. The ball must be dropped and come to rest not nearer the hole than the point where the original ball last crossed the margin of the hazard.

Note: *If a ball has been played from within a lateral water hazard and has not crossed any margin of the hazard, the player may drop a ball outside the hazard under Rule 33-3b.*

PENALTY FOR BREACH OF RULE:
Match play—Loss of hole; *Stroke play—Two strokes.

*Note 1: *In stroke play, in the event of a serious breach of Rule 33, see Rules 21-3c and 21-3d.*

Note 2: *It is a question of fact whether a ball lost after having been struck toward a water hazard is lost inside or outside the hazard. In order to treat the ball as lost in the hazard, there must be reasonable evidence that the ball lodged therein. In the absence of such evidence, the ball must be treated as a lost ball and Rule 29-1 applies.*

Rule 34
The Flagstick (Def. 12)

1. Flagstick Attended, Removed or Held up

Before and during the stroke, the player may have the flagstick attended, removed or held up to indicate the position of the hole. This may be done only on the authority of the player before he plays his stroke. If the flagstick be attended or removed by an opponent, a fellow-competitor or the caddie of either with the knowledge of the player and no objection is made, the player shall be deemed to have authorized it.

If a player or a caddie attend or remove the flagstick or stand near the hole while a stroke is being played, he shall be deemed to attend the flagstick until the ball comes to rest.

If the flagstick be not attended before the stroke is played, it shall not be attended or removed while the ball is in motion.

2. Unauthorized Attendance

a. MATCH PLAY

In match play, an opponent or his caddie shall not attend or remove the flagstick without the knowledge or authority of the player.

b. STROKE PLAY

In stroke play, if a fellow-competitor or his caddie attend or remove the flagstick without the knowledge or authority of the competitor, and if the ball strike the flagstick or the person attending it, it is a rub of the green, there is no penalty, and the ball shall be played as it lies.

PENALTY FOR BREACH OF RULE 34-1 AND -2:
Match play—Loss of hole; Stroke play—Two strokes.

3. Ball Striking Flagstick or Attendant

The player's ball shall not strike either:—

a. The flagstick when attended or removed by the player, his partner or either of their caddies, or by another person with the knowledge or authority of the player; or

b. The player's caddie, his partner or his partner's caddie when attending the flagstick, or another person attending the flagstick with the knowledge or authority of the player, or equipment carried by any such person; or

c. The flagstick in the hole, unattended, when the ball has been played from the putting green.

PENALTY FOR BREACH OF RULE 34-3:
Match play—Loss of hole; Stroke play—Two strokes, and the ball shall be played as it lies.

4. Ball Resting Against Flagstick

If the ball rest against the flagstick when it is in the hole, the player shall be entitled to have the flagstick removed, and if the ball fall into the hole the player shall be deemed to have holed out at his last stroke; otherwise, the ball, if moved, shall be placed on the lip of the hole, without penalty.

Rule 35
The Putting Green (Def. 25)

1. General

a. TOUCHING LINE OF PUTT

The line of the putt must not be touched except as provided in Clauses 1b, 1c and 1d of this Rule, or in measuring (Rule 20-1), or in removing movable obstructions (Rule 31-1), but the player may place the club in front of the ball in addressing it without pressing anything down.

b. LOOSE IMPEDIMENTS

The player may move sand, loose soil or any loose impediments on the putting green by picking them up or brushing them aside with his hand or a club without pressing anything down. If the ball be moved, it shall be replaced, without penalty.

c. REPAIR OF HOLE PLUGS AND BALL MARKS

The player or his partner may repair an old hole plug or damage to the putting green caused by the impact of a ball. If the player's ball lie on the putting green, it may be lifted to permit repair and shall be replaced on the spot from which it was lifted; in match play the ball must be replaced immediately if the opponent so requests.

If a ball be moved during such repair, it shall be replaced, without penalty.

d. LIFTING AND CLEANING BALL

A ball lying on the putting green may be lifted, without penalty, cleaned if desired, and replaced on the spot from which it was lifted; in match play the ball must be replaced immediately if the opponent so requests.

e. DIRECTION FOR PUTTING

When the player's ball is on the putting green, the player's caddie, his partner or his partner's caddie may, before the stroke is played, point out a line for putting, but the line of the putt shall not be touched in front of, to the side of, or behind the hole.

While making the stroke, the player shall not allow his caddie, his partner or his partner's caddie to position himself on or close to an extension of the line of putt behind the hole.

No mark shall be placed anywhere on the putting green to indicate a line for putting.

f. TESTING SURFACE

During the play of a hole, a player shall not test the surface of the putting green by rolling a ball or roughening or scraping the surface.

g. OTHER BALL TO BE AT REST

While the player's ball is in motion after a stroke on the putting green, an opponent's or a fellow-competitor's ball shall not be played or touched.

h. BALL IN MOTION STOPPED OR DEFLECTED

If a ball in motion after a stroke on the putting green be stopped or deflected by, or lodge in, any moving or animate outside agency, the stroke shall be cancelled and the ball shall be replaced.

Note: *If the referee or the Committee determine that a ball has been deliberately stopped or deflected by an outside agency, including a fellow-competitor or his caddie, further procedure should be prescribed in equity under Rule 11-4.*

i. BALL OVERHANGING HOLE

When any part of the ball overhangs the edge of the hole, the owner of the ball is not allowed more than a few seconds to determine whether it is at rest. If by then the ball has not fallen into the hole, it is deemed to be at rest.

j. BALL ON A WRONG PUTTING GREEN

If a ball lie on a putting green other than that of the hole being played, the point nearest to where the ball lies shall be determined which (a) is not nearer the hole and (b) is not in a hazard or on a putting green. The player shall lift the ball and drop it without penalty within one club-length of the point thus determined on ground which fulfils (a) and (b) above.

Note: *Unless otherwise stipulated by the Committee, the term "a putting green other than that of the hole being played" includes a practice putting or pitching green lying within the boundaries of the course.*

k. BALL TO BE MARKED WHEN LIFTED

Before a ball on the putting green is lifted, its position shall be marked. If the player fail so to mark the position of the ball, *the player shall incur a penalty of one stroke* and the ball shall be replaced.

(Lifting and placing—Rule 22.)

Note: *The position of a lifted ball should be marked by placing a ball-marker or other small object on the putting green, immediately behind the ball. If the marker interfere with the play, stance or stroke of another player, it should be placed one or more putterhead-lengths to one side.*

L. STANDING ASTRIDE OR ON LINE OF PUTT PROHIBITED

The player shall not make a stroke on the putting green from a stance astride, or with either foot touching, the line of the putt or an extension of that line behind the ball. For the purpose of Rule 35-1L only, the line of putt does not extend beyond the hole.

PENALTY FOR BREACH OF RULE 35-1:

Match play—Loss of hole; Stroke play—Two strokes.

2. Match Play

a. BALL INTERFERING WITH PLAY

When the player's ball lies on the putting green, if the player consider that the opponent's ball interfere with his play, he may require that the opponent's ball be lifted. The opponent's ball shall be replaced after the player has played his stroke. If the player's ball stop on the spot formerly occupied by the lifted ball, the player shall first play another stroke before the lifted ball is replaced.

If a ball be accidentally moved in complying with this Rule, no penalty shall be incurred and the ball shall be replaced.

b. PLAYING OUT OF TURN

If a player play when his opponent should have done so, the opponent may immediately require the player to replay the stroke, in which case the player shall replace his ball and play in correct order, without penalty.

c. OPPONENT'S BALL DISPLACED

If the player's ball knock the opponent's ball into the hole, the opponent shall be deemed to have holed out at his last stroke.

If the player's ball move the opponent's ball, the opponent may replace it, but this must be done before another stroke is played by either side. If the player's ball stop on the spot formerly occupied by the opponent's ball, and the opponent declare his intention to replace his ball, the player shall first play another stroke, after which the opponent shall replace his ball.

(Three-Ball, Best-Ball and Four-Ball match play—Rule 40-1c.)

d. CONCEDING OPPONENT'S NEXT STROKE

When the opponent's ball has come to rest, the player may concede the opponent to have holed out with his next stroke and may remove the opponent's ball with a club or otherwise. If the player does not concede the opponent's next stroke and the opponent's ball fall into the hole, the opponent shall be deemed to have holed out with his last stroke.

If the opponent's next stroke has not been conceded, the opponent shall play without delay in correct order.

PENALTY FOR BREACH OF RULE 35-2: *Loss of hole.*

3. Stroke Play

a. BALL INTERFERING WITH PLAY

When the competitor's ball lies on the putting green, if the competitor consider that a fellow-competitor's ball interfere with his play, he may require that the fellow-competitor's ball be lifted or played, at the fellow-competitor's option.

If a ball be accidentally moved in complying with this Rule, no penalty shall be incurred and the ball shall be replaced.

Note: *It is recommended that the interfering ball be played rather than lifted, unless the subsequent play of a fellow-competitor is likely to be affected.*

b. BALL ASSISTING PLAY

If the fellow-competitor consider that his ball lying on the putting green might be of assistance to the competitor, the fellow-competitor may lift or play first, without penalty.

c. BALL STRIKING FELLOW-COMPETITOR'S BALL

When both balls lie on the putting green, if the competitor's ball strike a fellow-competitor's ball, the *competitor shall incur a penalty of two strokes* and shall play his ball as it lies. The fellow-competitor's ball shall be at once replaced.

d. BALL LIFTED BEFORE HOLED OUT

For ball lifted before holed out, see Rules 7-2, 27-1c and 35-1k.

Rule 36
The Committee (Def. 9)

1. Conditions

The Committee shall lay down the conditions under which a competition is to be played.

Certain special rules governing stroke play are so substantially different from those governing match play that combining the two forms of play is not practicable and is not permitted. The results of matches played and the scores returned in these circumstances shall not be accepted.

2. Order and Times of Starting

a. GENERAL

The Committee shall arrange the order and times of starting.

b. MATCH PLAY

When a competition is played over an extended period, the Committee shall lay down the limit of time within which each round shall be completed.

When players are allowed to arrange the date of their match within these limits, the Committee should announce that the match must be played at a stated hour on the last day of the period unless the players agree to a prior date.

c. STROKE PLAY

Competitors shall play in couples unless the Committee authorizes play by threes or fours. If there be a single competitor, the Committee shall provide him with a player who shall mark for him, or provide a marker and allow him to compete alone, or allow him to compete with another group.

3. Decision of Ties

The Committee shall announce the manner, day and time for the decision of a halved match or of a tie, whether played on level terms or under handicap.

A halved match shall not be decided by stroke play. A tie in stroke play shall not be decided by a match.

4. The Course

a. NEW HOLES

New holes should be made on the day on which a stroke competition begins, and at such other times as the Committee considers necessary, provided all competitors in a single round play with each hole cut in the same position.

b. PRACTICE GROUND

Where there is no practice ground available outside the area of a competition course, the Committee should lay down the area on which players may practice on any day of a competition, if it is practicable to do so. On any day of a stroke competition, the Committee should not normally permit practice on or to a putting green or from a hazard of the competition course.

c. COURSE UNPLAYABLE

If the Committee or its authorized representative consider that for any reason the course is not in a playable condition, or that there are circumstances which render the proper playing of the game impossible, it shall have the power in match and stroke play to order a temporary suspension of play, or in stroke play to declare play null and void and to cancel all scores for the round in question.

When a round is cancelled, all penalties incurred in that round are cancelled.

When play has been temporarily suspended, it shall be resumed from where it was discontinued, even though resumption occur on a subsequent day.

(Procedure in discontinuing play—Rule 37-6b.)

5. Modification of Penalty

The Committee has no power to waive a Rule of Golf. A penalty of disqualification, however, may, in exceptional individual cases, be waived or be modified or be imposed if the Committee consider such action warranted.

6. Defining Bounds and Margins

The Committee shall define accurately:—
   a. The course and out of bounds.
   b. The margins of water hazards and lateral water hazards.
   c. Ground under repair.
   d. Obstructions.

7. Local Rules

a. POLICY

The Committee shall make and publish Local Rules for abnormal conditions, having regard to the policy of the Governing Authority of the country concerned as set forth in Appendix I attached to these Rules.

b. WAIVING PENALTY PROHIBITED

A penalty imposed by a Rule of Golf shall not be waived by a Local Rule.

Rule 37
The Player

1. Conditions

The player shall be responsible for acquainting himself with the conditions under which the competition is to be played.

2. Caddie

For any breach of a Rule or Local Rule by his caddie, the player incurs the relative penalty.

The player may have only one caddie, *under penalty of disqualification.*

The player may send his own caddie forward to mark the position of any ball.

3. Forecaddie

If a forecaddie be employed by the Committee, he is an outside agency (Def. 22).

4. Handicap

Before starting in a handicap competition, the player shall ensure that his current handicap is recorded correctly on the official list, if any, for the competition and on the card issued for him by the Committee. In the case of match play or bogey, par or Stableford competitions, he shall inform himself of the holes at which strokes are given or taken.

If a player play off a higher handicap than his current one, *he shall be disqualified* from the handicap competition. If he play off a lower one, the score, or the result of the match, shall stand.

5. Time and Order of Starting

The player shall start at the time and in the order arranged by the Committee.

PENALTY FOR BREACH OF RULE 37-5: *Disqualification.*

6. Discontinuance of Play

a. WHEN PERMITTED

The player shall not discontinue play on account of bad weather or for any other reason, unless:—

He considers that there be danger from lightning,

or

There be some other reason, such as sudden illness, which the Committee considers satisfactory.

If the player discontinue play without specific permission from the Committee, he shall report to the Committee as soon as possible.

General Exception:—Players discontinuing match play by agreement are not subject to disqualification unless by so doing the competition is delayed.

PENALTY FOR BREACH OF RULE 37-6a: *Disqualification.*

b. PROCEDURE

When play is discontinued in accordance with the Rules, it should, if feasible, be discontinued after the completion of the play of a hole. If this is not feasible, the player should lift his ball after marking the spot on which it lay; in such case he shall place a ball on that spot when play is resumed.

PENALTY FOR BREACH OF RULE 37-6b:

Match play—Loss of hole; *Stroke play—Two strokes.

*Note: *In stroke play, in the event of a serious breach of Rule 37-6b, see Rules 21-3c and 21-3d.*

7. Undue Delay

The player shall at all times play without undue delay. Between the completion of a hole and driving off the next tee, the player may not delay play in any way.

PENALTY FOR BREACH OF RULE 37-7:

*Match play—Loss of hole; Stroke play—Two strokes.

For repeated offense—Disqualification.

*If the player delay play between holes, he is delaying the play of the next hole, and the penalty applies to that hole.

8. Refusal to Comply with Rule

If a competitor in stroke play refuse to comply with a Rule affecting the rights of another competitor, *he shall be disqualified.*

9. Artificial Devices

Except as provided for under the Rules, the player shall not use any artificial device:—

a. Which might assist him in making a stroke or in his play;

b. For the purpose of gauging or measuring distance or conditions which might affect his play, or

c. Which, not being part of the grip (see Appendix IId), is designed to give him artificial aid in gripping the club.

(Exceptions to Rule 37-9c: Plain gloves and material or substance applied to the grip, such as tape, gauze or resin.)

PENALTY FOR BREACH OF RULE 37-9: *Disqualification.*

Rule 38
Scoring in Stroke Play

1. Recording Scores

The Committee shall issue for each competitor a score card containing the date and the competitor's name.

After each hole the marker should check the score with the competitor. On completion of the round the marker shall sign the card and hand it to the competitor; should more than one marker record the scores, each shall sign the part for which he is responsible.

2. Checking Scores

The competitor shall check his score for each hole, settle any doubtful points with the Committee, ensure that the marker has signed the card, countersign the card himself, and return it to the Committee as soon as possible. The competitor is solely responsible for the correctness of the score recorded for each hole.

PENALTY FOR BREACH OF RULE 38-2: *Disqualification.*

The Committee is responsible for the addition of scores and application of the handicap recorded on the card.

Exception: Four-ball stroke play—Rule 41-1d.

3. No Alteration of Scores

No alteration may be made on a card after the competitor has returned it to the Committee.

If the competitor return a score for any hole lower than actually taken, *he shall be disqualified.*

A score higher than actually taken must stand as returned.

Exception:—Four-ball stroke play—Rule 41-8a.

Rule 39
Bogey, Par or Stableford Competitions

1. Conditions

A bogey, par or Stableford competition is a form of stroke competition in which play is against a fixed score at each hole of the stipulated round or rounds.

a. The reckoning for bogey or par competitions is made as in match play. The winner is the competitor who is most successful in the aggregate of holes.

b. The reckoning in Stableford competitions is made by points awarded in relation to a fixed score at each hole as follows:—

For hole done in one over fixed score . . . . 1 point
For hole done in fixed score . . . . 2 points
For hole done in one under fixed score . . . . 3 points
For hole done in two under fixed score . . . . 4 points
For hole done in three under fixed score . . . . 5 points

The winner is the competitor who scores the highest number of points.

2. Rules for Stroke Play Apply

The Rules for stroke play shall apply with the following modifications:—

a. NO RETURN AT ANY HOLE

Any hole for which a competitor makes no return shall be regarded as a loss in bogey and par competitions and as scoring no points in Stableford competitions.

b. SCORING CARDS

The holes at which strokes are to be given or taken shall be indicated on the card issued by the Committee.

c. RECORDING SCORES

In bogey and par competitions the marker shall be responsible for marking only the gross number of strokes for each hole where the competitor makes a net score equal to or less than the fixed score. In Stableford competitions the marker shall be responsible for marking only the gross number of strokes at each hole where the competitor's net score earns one or more points.

Note: *Maximum of 14 Clubs—see Rule 3-2 and Rule 41-7.*

3. Disqualification Penalties

a. FROM THE COMPETITION

A competitor shall be disqualified from the competition for a breach of any of the following:

Rule 2—The Club and the Ball.
Rule 4—Agreement to Waive Rules Prohibited.
Rule 8-3—Practice before Round.
Rule 35-3a—Putting Green: Stroke Play, Ball Interfering with Play.
Rule 37-2—Caddie.
Rule 37-4—Handicap (playing off higher handicap than current one).
Rule 37-5—Time and Order of Starting.
Rule 37-6a—Discontinuance of Play.
Rule 37-7—Undue Delay (repeated offense).
Rule 37-8—Refusal to Comply with Rule.
Rule 37-9—Artificial Devices.
Rule 38-2—Checking Scores.
Rule 38-3—No Alteration of Scores, except that the competitor shall not be disqualified when a breach of this Rule does not affect the result of the hole.

b. FOR A HOLE

In all other cases where a breach of a Rule would entail disqualification, *the competitor shall be disqualified only for the hole at which the breach occurred.*

(Modification of penalty—Rule 36-5.)

Rule 40
Three-Ball, Best-Ball and Four-Ball Match Play

1. General

a. RULES OF GOLF APPLY

The Rules of Golf, so far as they are not at variance with the following special Rules, shall apply to all three-ball, best-ball and four-ball matches.

b. BALL INFLUENCING PLAY

Any player may have any ball (except the ball about to be played) lifted if he consider that it might interfere with or be of assistance to a player or side, but this may not be done while any ball in the match is in motion.

c. BALL MOVED BY ANOTHER BALL

There is no penalty if a player's ball move any other ball in the match. The owner of the moved ball shall replace his ball.

d. PLAYING OUT OF TURN

On the teeing ground, if a player play when an opponent should have played, the opponent may immediately require the player to abandon the ball so played and to play a ball in correct order, without penalty.

Through the green or in a hazard, a player shall incur no penalty if he play when an opponent should have done so. The stroke shall not be replayed.

On the putting green, if a player play when an opponent should have done so, the opponent may immediately require the player to replay the stroke in correct order, without penalty.

2. Three-Ball Match Play

In a three-ball match, each player is playing two distinct matches.

a. BALL STOPPED OR DEFLECTED BY AN OPPONENT ACCIDENTALLY

If a player's ball be accidentally stopped or deflected by an opponent, his caddie or equipment, no penalty shall be incurred. In his match with that opponent, the player may play the ball as it lies or, before another stroke is played by either side, he may cancel the stroke, place a ball on the spot where the ball previously lay and replay the stroke. In his match with the other opponent, the occurrence shall be treated as a rub of the green (Def. 27) and the hole shall be played out with the original ball.

Exception:—Ball striking person attending flagstick—Rule 34-3b.

(Ball purposely stopped or deflected by opponent—Rule 17-4.)
b. BALL AT REST MOVED BY AN OPPONENT

If the player's ball be touched or moved by an opponent, his caddie or equipment (except as otherwise provided in the Rules), Rule 27-2a applies. *That opponent shall incur a penalty stroke in his match with the player,* but not in his match with the other opponent.

3. Best-Ball and Four-Ball Match Play

a. ORDER OF PLAY

Balls belonging to the same side may be played in the order the side considers best.

b. BALL STOPPED BY PLAYER'S SIDE

If a player's ball be stopped or deflected by the player, his partner or either of their caddies or equipment, *the player is disqualified for the hole.* His partner incurs no penalty.

c. BALL STOPPED BY OPPONENT'S SIDE ACCIDENTALLY

If a player's ball be accidentally stopped or deflected by an opponent, his caddie or equipment, no penalty shall be incurred. The player may play the ball as it lies or, before another stroke is played by either side, he may cancel the stroke, place a ball on the spot where the ball previously lay and replay the stroke.

Exception:—Ball striking person attending flagstick—Rule 34-3b.

(Ball purposely stopped or deflected by opponent—Rule 17-4.)
d. WRONG BALL

If a player play a stroke with a wrong ball (Def. 5) except in a hazard, *he shall be disqualified for that hole,* but the penalty shall not apply to his partner. If the wrong ball belong to another player, its owner shall place a ball on the spot from which the wrong ball was played, without penalty.

e. PARTNER'S BALL MOVED BY PLAYER ACCIDENTALLY

If a player, his partner, or either of their caddies accidentally move a ball owned by their side or by touching anything cause it to move (except as otherwise provided for in the Rules), *the owner of the ball shall incur a penalty stroke,* but the penalty shall not apply to his partner. The ball shall be replaced.

f. BALL MOVED BY OPPONENT'S SIDE

If a player's ball be touched or moved by an opponent, his caddie or equipment (except as otherwise provided in the Rules), *that opponent shall incur a penalty stroke,* but the penalty shall not apply to the other opponent. The player shall replace the ball, without penalty.

g. MAXIMUM OF FOURTEEN CLUBS

The side shall be penalized for a violation of Rule 3 by either partner.

h. DISQUALIFICATION PENALTIES

A player shall be disqualified from the match for a breach of Rule 37-5 (Time and Order of Starting), but, in the discretion of the Committee, the penalty shall not necessarily apply to his partner (Definition 28—Note).

A side shall be disqualified for a breach of any of the following:—

Rule 2—The Club and the Ball.
Rule 4—Agreement to Waive Rules Prohibited.
Rule 37-2—Caddie.
Rule 37-4—Handicap (playing off higher handicap than current one).
Rule 37-7—Undue Delay (repeated offense).
Rule 37-9—Artificial Devices.

A player shall be disqualified for the hole in question and from the remainder of the match for a breach of Rule 37-6a (Discontinuance of Play), but the penalty shall not apply to his partner.
(Modification of penalty—Rule 36-5.)

i. INFRINGEMENT ASSISTING PARTNER OR AFFECTING OPPONENT

If a player's infringement of a Rule or Local Rule assist his partner's play or adversely affect an opponent's play, *the partner incurs the relative penalty in addition to any penalty incurred by the player.*

j. PENALTY APPLIES TO PLAYER ONLY

In all other cases where, by the Rules or Local Rules, a player would incur a penalty, the penalty shall not apply to his partner.

k. ANOTHER FORM OF MATCH PLAYED CONCURRENTLY

In a best-ball or a four-ball match when another form of match is played concurrently, the above special Rules shall apply.

Rule 41
Four-Ball Stroke Play

1. Conditions

a. The Rules of Golf, so far as they are not at variance with the following special Rules, shall apply to four-ball stroke play.

b. In four-ball stroke play two competitors play as partners, each playing his own ball.

c. The lower score of the partners is the score of the hole.

If one partner fail to complete the play of a hole, there is no penalty.
(Wrong score—Rule 41-8a.)

d. The marker is required to record for each hole only the gross score of whichever partner's score is to count. The partners are responsible for the correctness of only their gross scores for each hole. The Committee is responsible for recording the better-ball score for each hole, the addition and the application of the handicaps recorded on the card.

e. Only one of the partners need be responsible for complying with Rule 38.

2. Ball Influencing Play

Any competitor may have any ball (except the ball about to be played) lifted or played, at the option of the owner, if he consider that it might interfere with or be of assistance to a competitor or side, but this may not be done while any ball in the group is in motion.

If the owner of the ball refuse to comply with this Rule when required to do so, *his side shall be disqualified.*

3. Balls to be at Rest

While the competitor's ball is in motion after a stroke on the putting green, any other ball shall not be played or touched.

4. Ball Struck by Another Ball

When the balls concerned lie on the putting green, if a competitor's ball strike any other ball, *the competitor shall incur a penalty of two strokes* and shall play his ball as it lies. The other ball shall be at once replaced.

In all other cases, if a competitor's ball strike any other ball, the competitor shall play his ball as it lies. The owner of the moved ball shall replace his ball, without penalty.

5. Order of Play

Balls belonging to the same side may be played in the order the side considers best.

6. Wrong Ball

If a competitor play any strokes with a wrong ball (Def. 5) except in a hazard, *he shall add two penalty strokes* to his score for the hole and then play the correct ball (Rule 21-3).

If the wrong ball belong to another player its owner shall place a ball on the spot from which the wrong ball was played, without penalty.

7. Maximum of Fourteen Clubs

The side shall be penalized for a violation of Rule 3 by either partner.

8. Disqualification Penalties

a. FROM THE COMPETITION

A competitor shall be disqualified from the competition for a breach of any of the following, but the penalty shall not apply to his partner:—

Rule 8-3—Practice before Round.
Rule 37-5—Time and Order of Starting.

A side shall be disqualified from the competition for a breach of any of the following:—

Rule 2—The Club and the Ball.
Rule 4—Agreement to Waive Rules Prohibited.
Rule 37-2—Caddie.
Rule 37-4—Handicap (playing off higher handicap than current one).
Rule 37-7—Undue Delay (repeated offense).
Rule 37-8—Refusal to Comply with Rule.
Rule 37-9—Artificial Devices.
Rule 38-2—Checking Scores.
Rule 38-3—No alteration of scores, i.e., when the recorded lower score of the partners is lower than actually played. If the recorded lower score of the partners is higher than actually played, it must stand as returned.
Rule 41-2—Ball Influencing Play, Refusal to Lift.

By both partners, at the same hole, of a Rule or Rules the penalty for which is disqualification either from the competition or for a hole.

b. FROM THE REMAINDER OF THE COMPETITION

A competitor shall be disqualified for the hole in question and from the remainder of the competition for a breach of Rule 37-6a (Discontinuance of Play), but the penalty shall not apply to his partner.

c. FOR THE HOLE ONLY

In all other cases where a breach of a Rule would entail disqualification, *the competitor shall be disqualified only for the hole at which the breach occurred.*

(Modification of penalty—Rule 36-5.)

9. Infringement Assisting Partner

If a competitor's infringement of a Rule or Local Rule assist his partner's play, *the partner incurs the relative penalty in addition to any penalty incurred by the competitor.*

10. Penalty Applies to Competitor Only

In all other cases where, by the Rules or Local Rules, a competitor would incur a penalty, the penalty shall not apply to his partner.

Appendix I
LOCAL RULES

Rule 36-7 provides:

"The Committee shall make and publish Local Rules for abnormal conditions, having regard to the policy of the Governing Authority of the country concerned as set forth in Appendix I attached to these Rules.

"A penalty imposed by a Rule of Golf shall not be waived by a Local Rule."

Among the matters for which Local Rules or other regulations may be advisable are the following:

1. Lateral Water Hazards

Clarifying the status of sections of water hazards which may be lateral under Definition 14c and Rule 33-3.

2. Obstructions

a CLARIFYING STATUS: Clarifying the status of objects which may be obstructions under Definition 20 and Rule 31.

b. WHEN INTEGRAL PART OF COURSE: Declaring not an obstruction any construction which the Committee considers an integral part of the course (Definition 20c); e.g., built-up sides and surfaces of teeing grounds, putting greens and bunkers.

3. Defining Bounds and Margins

Specifying means used to define out of bounds, hazards, water hazards, lateral water hazards, and ground under repair.

4. Ball Drops

Establishment of special areas on which balls may be dropped when it is not feasible to proceed exactly in conformity with Rule 29-2b (ball unplayable), Rule 31-2b (immovable obstruction) and Rules 33-2,-3 (water hazards and lateral water hazards).

5. Provisional Ball, Water Hazard

Permitting play of a provisional ball for a ball which may be in a water hazard of such character that it would be impracticable to determine whether the ball is in the hazard or to do so would unduly delay play. In such case, if a provisional ball is played and the original ball is in a water hazard, the player may play the original ball as it lies or continue the provisional ball in play, but he may not proceed under Rule 33-2 or 33-3.

6. Preservation of Course

Preservation of the course, including turf nurseries and other parts of the course under cultivation on which play is prohibited.

7. Temporary Conditions—Mud, Extreme Wetness

Temporary conditions which might interfere with proper playing of the game, including mud and extreme wetness warranting lifting an embedded ball anywhere through the green on specific individual days *(see detailed recommendation below)* or removal of mud from a ball through the green.

8. Accumulation of Leaves

9. Unusual Damage To the Course (other than as covered in Rule 32.)

10. Roads and Paths

Providing relief of the type afforded under Rule 31-2b from roads and paths not having artificial surfaces and sides if they could unfairly affect play.

11. Priority On the Course (see Etiquette)

12. Practice Areas (see Rules 8 and 36-4b)

13. Automotive Transport

Specifying whether automotive transportation may or may not be used by players.

Lifting an Embedded Ball

Rule 16-2 provides relief without penalty for a ball embedded in its own pitch-mark in any closely mown area through the green.

On the putting green, Rule 35-1c permits a ball to be lifted to repair damage caused by the impact of a ball.

When permission to lift an embedded ball anywhere through the green (Definition 35) would be warranted on specific individual days, the following Local Rule is suggested:

Anywhere "through the green," a ball which is embedded in its own pitch-mark in ground other than sand may be lifted without penalty, cleaned, and dropped as near as possible to the spot where it lay but not nearer the hole. *(See Rule 22.)*
("Through the green" (Definition 35) is the whole area of the course except:—
a. Teeing ground and putting green of the hole being played;
b. All hazards on the course.)

Practice at Putting Green of Hole Played

When it is desired to prohibit practice on or to a putting green of a hole already played, the following Local Rule is recommended:

A player during a round shall not play any practice stroke on or to the putting green of any hole he has played in the round. (For other practice, see Rules 8 and 36-4b.)
PENALTY FOR BREACH OF LOCAL RULE:
Match play—Loss of hole; Stroke play—Two strokes.

Marking Position of Lifted Ball

When it is desired to require a specific means of marking the position of a lifted ball on the putting green, the following Local Rule is recommended:

Before a ball on the putting green is lifted, its position shall be marked by placing an object, such as a small coin, immediately behind the ball; if the object interfere with another player, it should be moved one or more putterhead-lengths to one side. If the player fail so to mark the position of the ball, *the player shall incur a penalty of one stroke* and the ball shall be replaced. (This modifies Rule 35-1k.)
PENALTY FOR BREACH OF LOCAL RULE:
Match play—Loss of hole; Stroke play—Two strokes.

Prohibition against
Touching Line of Putt with Club

When it is desired to prohibit touching the line of putt with a club in moving loose impediments, the following Local Rule is recommended:

The line of putt shall not be touched with a club for any purpose except to repair old hole plugs or ball marks or during address. (This modifies Rule 35-1b.)
PENALTY FOR BREACH OF LOCAL RULE:
Match play—Loss of hole; Stroke play—Two strokes.

Temporary Obstructions

When temporary obstructions are installed for a competition, the following Local Rule is recommended:

1. Definition

Temporary immovable obstructions include tents, scoreboards, grandstands, refreshment stands, lavatories and, provided it is not mobile or otherwise readily movable, any piece of equipment for photography, press, radio, television and scoring services.

Excluded are temporary power lines and cables (from which relief is provided in Clause 4) and mobile or otherwise readily movable equipment for photography, press, etc. (from which relief is obtainable under Rule 31-1).

2. Interference

Interference by a temporary immovable obstruction occurs when (a) the ball lies in or on the obstruction or so close to the obstruction that the obstruction interferes with the player's stance or the area of his intended swing or (b) the obstruction intervenes between the player's ball and the hole or the ball lies within one club-length of a spot where such intervention would exist.

However, if it is not reasonable for the player to play a stroke toward the flagstick because of interference by anything other than a temporary obstruction, he may not apply Clause 3a or 3b below.

3. Relief

A player may obtain relief from interference by a temporary immovable obstruction, without penalty, as follows:—

a. THROUGH THE GREEN

Through the green, the point nearest to where the ball lies shall be determined which (a) is not nearer the hole, (b) avoids interference as defined in Clause 2 of this Local Rule and (c) is not in a hazard or on a putting green. He shall lift the ball and drop it within one club-length of the point thus determined on ground which fulfils (a), (b) and (c) above. The ball may be cleaned, without penalty, when so lifted.

b. IN A HAZARD

If the ball lie in a hazard, a ball shall be dropped either:

(i) In the hazard, without penalty, on the nearest ground affording complete relief within the limits specified in Clause 3a above or, if complete relief is impossible, on ground within the hazard affording maximum relief, or

(ii) Outside the hazard, under penalty of one stroke, as follows: The player shall determine the point nearest to where the ball lies which (a) is not nearer the hole, (b) avoids interference as defined in Clause 2 of this Local Rule and (c) is not in the hazard. He shall drop the ball within one club-length of the point thus determined on ground which fulfils (a), (b) and (c) above.

4. Temporary Power Lines and Cables

The above Clauses do not apply to temporary power lines and cables. If such lines and cables are readily movable, the player may obtain relief under Rule 31-1. If they are not readily movable, the player may obtain relief under Rule 31-2.

If a ball strikes an elevated power line or cable, it must be replaced and replayed, without penalty. (Exception: Ball striking elevated junction section of cable rising from the ground shall not be replayed.)

5. Re-Dropping

If a dropped ball roll into a position covered by this Local Rule, or nearer the hole than its original position, it shall be re-dropped without penalty. If it again roll into such a position, it shall be placed where it first struck the ground when re-dropped.

PENALTY FOR BREACH OF LOCAL RULE
Match play—Loss of hole; Stroke play—Two strokes.

"Preferred Lies" and "Winter Rules"

The USGA does not endorse "preferred lies" and "winter rules," and recommends that the Rules of Golf be observed uniformly. Ground under repair is provided for in Definition 13 and Rule 32. Occasional abnormal conditions which might interfere with fair play and are not widespread should be defined accurately as ground under repair.

However, adverse conditions are sometimes so general throughout a course that the local Committee believes "preferred lies" or "winter rules" would promote fair and pleasant play or help protect the course. Heavy snows, spring thaws, prolonged rains or extreme heat can make fairways unsatisfactory and sometimes prevent use of heavy mowing equipment.

When a Committee adopts a local rule for "preferred lies" or "winter rules," it should be in detail and should be interpreted by the Committee, as there is no established code for "winter rules." Without a detailed local rule, it is meaningless for a Committee to post a notice merely saying "Winter Rules Today."

The following local rule would seem appropriate for the conditions in question, but the USGA does not endorse it and will not interpret it:

A ball lying on a "fairway" may be lifted and cleaned, with-out penalty, and placed within six inches of where it originally lay, not nearer the hole, and so as to preserve as nearly as possible the stance required to play from the original lie. After the ball has been so placed, it is in play, and if it move after the player has addressed it *the penalty shall be one stroke*—see Rule 27-1f.

If the adverse conditions extend onto the putting green, the above local rule may be altered by adding the words "or the putting green" after the word "fairway."

If it is desired to *protect* the course, the above local rule should be reworded to make it mandatory rather than permissive to move the ball from certain areas. The above rule does not require a player to move his ball if he does not want to do so.

Before a Committee adopts a local rule permitting "preferred lies" or "winter rules," the following facts should be considered:

1. Such a local rule conflicts with the Rules of Golf and the fundamental principle of playing the ball as it lies.

2. "Winter rules" are sometimes adopted under the guise of protecting the course when, in fact, the practical effect is just the opposite—they permit moving the ball to the best turf, from which divots are then taken to injure the course further.

3. "Preferred lies" or "winter rules" tend generally to lower scores and handicaps, thus penalizing the players in competition with players whose scores for handicaps are made under the Rules of Golf.

4. Extended use or indiscriminate use of "preferred lies" or "winter rules" will place players at a disadvantage when competing at a course where the ball must be played as it lies.

Handicapping and "Preferred Lies"

Scores made under a local rule for "preferred lies" or "winter rules" may be accepted for handicapping if the Committee considers that conditions warrant.

When such a local rule is adopted, the Committee should ensure that the course's normal scoring difficulty is maintained as nearly as possible through adjustment of tee markers and related methods. However, if extreme conditions cause extended use of "preferred lies" or "winter rules" and the course management cannot adjust scoring difficulty properly, the club should obtain a Temporary Course Rating from its district golf association.

Appendix II
DESIGN OF CLUBS (DEF. 36)

Rule 2-2a provides in part:—

"The golf club shall be composed of a shaft and a head, and all of the various parts shall be fixed so that the club is one unit; the club shall not be designed to be adjustable, except for weight.

"**Note:** *Playing characteristics not to be changed during a round—Rule 2-2b.*

"The club shall not be substantially different from the traditional and customary form and make, and shall conform with the regulations governing the design of clubs."

The following are the regulations governing the design of clubs:—

a. SHAPE OF HEAD

The length of a clubhead shall be greater than the breadth.

Length shall be determined on a horizontal line, five-eighths of an inch above the sole, from the back of the heel to the end of the toe or a vertical projection thereof.

Breadth shall be determined on a horizontal line between the outermost points of the face and the back of the head or vertical projections thereof.

b. FACE OF HEAD

The club shall have only one face designed for striking the ball, except that a putter may have two faces if the loft of both faces is substantially the same and does not exceed ten degrees.

Club faces shall not embody any degree of concavity on the hitting surface.

Club faces shall not have any lines, dots or other markings with sharp or rough edges, or any type of finish, for the purpose of unduly influencing the movement of the ball.

Markings on the face of a club shall conform with the specifications in Appendix III at page 60. The face of an iron club shall not contain an inset or attachment.

c. SHAFT

The shaft shall be designed to be straight from the top to a point not more than five inches above the sole. The shaft, including any inserted plug, shall be generally circular in cross-section and shall extend to the upper end of the grip.

The shaft shall be fixed to the clubhead at the heel (as illustrated in Figure A on page 58). The shaft may be attached directly to the clubhead or to a neck or socket of the clubhead; any neck or socket shall not be more than five inches in length measured from the top of the neck or socket to the sole. The shaft and the neck or socket shall remain in line with the heel, or with a point to right or left of the heel, when the club is soled at address. The distance between the axis of the shaft (or the neck or socket) and the back of the heel shall not exceed five-eighths of an inch in wood clubs and five-sixteenths of an inch in iron clubs.

Exception for Putters:—The shaft or neck or socket of a putter may be fixed at any point in the head and need not remain in line with the heel. The axis of the shaft from the top to a point not more than five inches above the sole shall diverge from the vertical by at least ten degrees in relation to the horizontal line determining length of head under Appendix IIa. The shaft in cross-section shall be generally circular or otherwise symmetrical.

d. GRIP

The grip consists of that part of the shaft designed to be held by the player and any material added to it for the purpose of obtain-

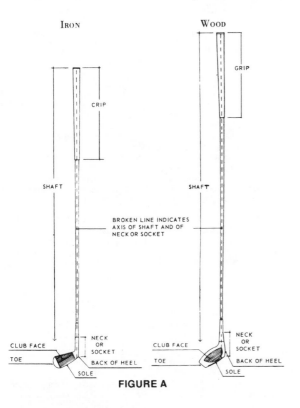

FIGURE A

ing a firm hold. The grip shall be substantially straight and plain in form, may have flat sides, but shall not have a channel or a furrow or be molded for any part of the hands.

The following are examples of grips which have been approved and some which have been disapproved:—

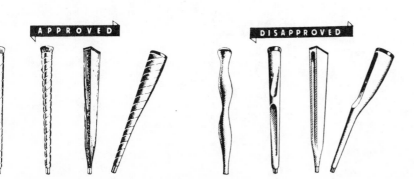

Appendix III
MARKINGS ON CLUBS (DEF. 36)

Rule 2-2a provides in part:—

"The golf club shall be composed of a shaft and a head, and all of the various parts shall be fixed so that the club is one unit; the club shall not be designed to be adjustable, except for weight.

"**Note:** *Playing characteristics not to be changed during a round—Rule 2-2b.*

"The club shall not be substantially different from the traditional and customary form and make, and shall conform with the regulations governing the design of clubs at Appendix II and the specifications for markings on clubs."

Appendix IIb provides in part:

"Club faces shall not have any lines, dots or other markings with sharp or rough edges, or any type of finish, for the purpose of unduly influencing the movement of the ball. Markings of the face of a club shall conform with the specifications."

Sharp or rough edges of markings may be determined by a finger test. A different problem is presented, however, by the detailed Specifications for Markings on Clubs. These are manufacturing specifications. For the guidance of players and Committees, following are a layman's interpretation of some essential parts of the specifications:

In general it is required that the face of a club shall present a smooth, flat surface on which a limited percentage of the area may be depressed by markings.

When the depressed area is in the form of grooves, each groove may not be wider than .035 inch (approximately one thirty-second of an inch), the angle between the flat surface of the club face and the side of the groove may not be less than 135 degrees. Except as provided elsewhere, the distance between grooves may not be less than three times the width of the groove.

When the depressed area is in the form of punch marks, the markings must not exceed .075 inch (a little over one-sixteenth of an inch) in diameter.

The complete specifications are:—

Specifications

In general a definite area of the surface is reserved for scoring. All the sections contained in this specification shall refer to this particular scored area. With regard to an iron club, reasonably-sized areas of the heel and the toe shall not be scored—see illustration of "Golf Head Scorings" below. This restriction does not apply to wood clubs.

This specification is divided into three sections: Section 1 refers to golf clubs where grooves are used; Section 2 refers to golf clubs scored with punch marks; Section 3 includes a combination of groove and punch markings.

Section 1-a Wood Clubs

Wood clubs shall not have any markings on the face for the purpose of unduly influencing the movement of the ball. Where the loft or face angle exceeds 24 degrees, grooves shall be generally straight with a maximum width measured in the face plane of .040 inches. The depth of any groove shall not be greater than 1½ times the width. At no place on the face shall the distance between the edges of the grooves be less than three times the width of the adjacent groove.

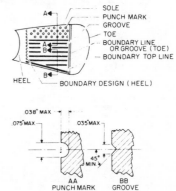

Golf Head Scorings

Section 1-b Iron Clubs

1. A series of straight grooves in the form of V's may be put in the face of the club. The side walls of the grooves shall be essentially flat and the included angle shall be equal to or greater than 90 degrees. The bisector of the angle shall be normal to the face of the club. (See illustration of "Golf Head Scorings.")

2. The width of a groove shall be generally consistent and not exceed .035 inches along its full length. This width shall be measured in the plane of the face of the club between the two points where the planes of the groove meet the face of the club. The widths of grooves in any club face shall be generally consistent.

3. At no place on the face of the club shall the distances between edges of the grooves be less than three times the width of a groove, with the minimum distance between the edges of any two grooves being .075 inches.

4. Lines may be used to define the toe, heel and top boundaries of the scored area. Such a line must be no wider or deeper than .040 inches. Designs may be used to indicate the toe and heel boundaries of the scored area. They must be no deeper than .040 inches. Designs and lines must have smooth edges and shall not be designed in any way to influence unduly the movement of the ball.

5. The scored area shall be considered as that portion of the face within boundary lines or designs. In the case where such lines or designs do not exist, the scored area shall be that portion between the extremities of the grooves.

6. The center or intended impact center of the face may be indicated by a design which shall fit within the boundary of a square whose sides are .375 inches in length. Such a marking shall not in any way be designed to influence unduly the movement of the ball.

7. The face of the club shall be smooth and flat over the full surface. No sharp edges or lips due to die impression of any type will be permitted. For decorative purposes only, it is permissible to sandblast the scored area not to exceed a roughness of 180 microinches, with 15% tolerance. The relative roughness shall be determined in accordance with USA standards (ASA B46.1-1962) for surface texture. The direction of measurement shall be parallel to the grooves.

The above conditions for smoothness apply also to Sections 2 and 3.

Section 2

Punch marks may be used in the place of grooves. The area of such a mark, in the plane of the face, may not exceed .0044 square inches. A mark may not be closer to an adjacent mark than 0.168 inches measured from center to center. The depth of a mark may not be greater than .038 inches with centerline normal to the face. Punchmarks must be evenly distributed throughout the scored area.

Section 3

In the event punch marks in combination with grooves are used within the scored area, groove specifications govern as in Section 1 if grooves are adjacent. Punch mark specifications govern if punch marks are adjacent. At no place may a punch mark be closer to a groove measured from center to center than .168 inches.

Appendix IV
MISCELLANEOUS
How to Decide Ties in Handicap Events

Rule 36-3 empowers the Committee to determine how and when a halved match or a stroke play tie shall be decided. The decision should be published in advance.

The USGA recommends:

1. Match Play

A handicap match which ends all even should be played off hole by hole until one side wins a hole. The play-off should start on the hole where the match began. Strokes should be allowed as in the prescribed round.

2. Stroke Play

A handicap stroke competition which ends in a tie should be played off at 18 holes, with handicaps. If a shorter play-off be necessary, the percentage of 18 holes to be played shall be applied to the players' handicaps to determine their play-off handicaps. It is advisable to arrange for a percentage of holes that will result in whole numbers in handicaps; if this is not feasible, handicap stroke fractions of one-half or more shall count as a full stroke, and any lesser fractions shall be disregarded. *Example:* In an individual competition, A's handicap is 10 and B's is 8. It would be appropriate to conduct a nine-hole play-off (50% of 18 holes) with A receiving 5 strokes and B 4 strokes.

Pairings for Match Play

General Numerical Draw

For purposes of determining places in the draw, ties in qualifying rounds other than those for the last qualifying place shall be decided by the order in which scores are returned, the first score to be returned receiving the lowest available number, etc. If it be impossible to determine the order in which scores are returned, ties shall be determined by a blind draw.

UPPER HALF	LOWER HALF	UPPER HALF	LOWER HALF
64 QUALIFIERS		32 QUALIFIERS	
1 vs. 33	2 vs. 34	1 vs. 17	2 vs. 18
17 vs. 49	18 vs. 50	9 vs. 25	10 vs. 26
9 vs. 41	10 vs. 42	5 vs. 21	6 vs. 22
25 vs. 57	26 vs. 58	13 vs. 29	14 vs. 30
5 vs. 37	6 vs. 38	3 vs. 19	4 vs. 20
21 vs. 53	22 vs. 54	11 vs. 27	12 vs. 28
13 vs. 45	14 vs. 46	7 vs. 23	8 vs. 24
29 vs. 61	30 vs. 62	15 vs. 31	16 vs. 32
3 vs. 35	4 vs. 36	16 QUALIFIERS	
19 vs. 51	20 vs. 52	1 vs. 9	2 vs. 10
11 vs. 43	12 vs. 44	5 vs. 13	6 vs. 14
27 vs. 59	28 vs. 60	3 vs. 11	4 vs. 12
7 vs. 39	8 vs. 40	7 vs. 15	8 vs. 16
23 vs. 55	24 vs. 56	8 QUALIFIERS	
15 vs. 47	16 vs. 48	1 vs. 5	2 vs. 6
31 vs. 63	32 vs. 64	3 vs. 7	4 vs. 8

Par Computation

"Par" is the score that an expert golfer would be expected to make for a given hole. Par means errorless play without flukes and under ordinary weather conditions, allowing two strokes on the putting green.

Yardages for guidance in computing par are given below. They are not arbitrary, because allowance should be made for the configuration of the ground, any difficult or unusual conditions, and the severity of the hazards.

Each hole should be measured horizontally from the middle of the tee area to be used to the center of the green, following the line of play planned by the architect in laying out the hole. Thus, in a hole with a bend, the line at the elbow point should be centered in the fairway in accordance with the architect's intention.

YARDAGES FOR GUIDANCE		
PAR	MEN	WOMEN
3	up to 250	up to 210
4	251 to 470	211 to 400
5	471 and over	401 to 575
6		576 and over

Handicapping

Par as computed above should not be confused with Course Rating as described in the USGA Golf Handicap System. USGA Handicaps must be based on Course Rating rather than par. See the booklet "Golf Committee Manual and USGA Golf Handicap System."

Flagstick Dimensions

The USGA recommends that the flagstick be at least seven feet in height and that its diameter be not greater than three-quarters of an inch from a point three inches above the ground to the bottom of the hole.

Protection of Persons against Lightning

As there have been many deaths and injuries from lightning on golf courses, all players, caddies, and sponsors of golf are urged to take every precaution for the protection of persons against lightning.

The National Bureau of Standards points out:

"If golf clubs could be impressed with the necessity of calling off matches *before the storm is near enough to be hazardous,* the cases of multiple injury or death among players and spectators could be eliminated."

Raising golf clubs or umbrellas above the head adds to the element of personal hazard during electrical storms.

Metal spikes on golf shoes do little to increase the hazard, according to the Bureau.

Taking Shelter

The following rules for personal safety during thunderstorms are based on material in the Lightning Protection Code, NFPA No. 78-1977; ANSI C5. 1-1975 available from the National Fire Protection Association, 470 Atlantic Ave., Boston, Mass. 02210, and the American National Standards Institute, 1430 Broadway, New York, N.Y. 10018:

(a) *Types of Shelter*

Do not go out of doors or remain out during thunderstorms unless it is necessary. Seek shelter inside buildings, vehicles, or other structures or locations which offer protection from lightning, such as:

1. Dwellings or other buildings protected against lightning.
2. Large metal-frame buildings.
3. Large unprotected buildings.
4. Automobiles with metal tops and bodies.
5. Trailers with metal bodies.
6. City streets shielded by nearby buildings.

When it is not possible to choose a location that offers better protection, seek shelter in:

1. Dense woods—avoid isolated trees.
2. Depressed areas—avoid hilltops and high places.
3. Small unprotected buildings, tents and shelters in *low* areas—avoid unprotected buildings and shelters in *high* areas.

(b) *What to Avoid*

Certain locations are extremely hazardous during thunderstorms and should be avoided if at all possible. Approaching thunderstorms should be anticipated and the following locations avoided when storms are in the immediate vicinity:

1. Open fields.
2. Athletic fields.
3. Golf courses.
4. Swimming pools, lakes and seashores.
5. Near wire fences, clotheslines, overhead wires and railroad tracks.
6. Isolated trees.
7. Hilltops and wide open spaces.

In the above locations, it is especially hazardous to be riding in or on any of the following during lightning storms:

1. Tractors and other farm machinery operated on the golf course for maintenance of same.
2. Golf carts, scooters, motorcycles, bicycles.

Discontinuing Play during Lightning

Attention is called to Rules 36-4c, 37-5 and 37-6.

The USGA especially suggests that players be informed that they have the right to stop play if they think lightning threatens them, even though the Committee may not have specifically authorized it by signal.

The USGA uses the following signals and recommends that all local committees do similarly:

Discontinue Play: Three consecutive notes of siren, repeated.

Resume Play: One prolonged note of siren, repeated.

Lightning Protection for Shelters

Shelters on golf courses may best be protected by standard lightning protection systems. Details on the installation of conductors, air terminals, and maintenance requirements are included in the Lightning Protection Code.

An alternate method of protection of such shelters is through what is known as providing a "cone of protection" with grounded rods or masts and overhead conductors as described in Section 31 of the Lightning Protection Code. Such a system is feasible for small structures, but probably would be more expensive than a standard lightning rod system.

Down conductors should be shielded with non-conductive material, resistant to impact and climatic conditions to a height of approximately 8 feet to protect persons from contact with down conductors. Shelters with earthen floors which are provided with lightning protection systems should have any approved grounding electrodes interconnected by an encircling buried, bare conductor of a type suitable for such service, or such electrodes should be provided with radial conductors run out to a distance of at least 10 feet from the electrode, away from the shelter.

★   ★   ★

It is recommended that several notices similar to this be posted at every course. Copies of this notice in poster form may be obtained from the USGA.

Rules of Amateur Status

Any person who considers that any action he is proposing to take might endanger his amateur status should submit particulars to the United States Golf Association for consideration.

Definition of an Amateur Golfer

An amateur golfer is one who plays the game as a non-remunerative or non-profit-making sport.

Rule 1
Forfeiture of Amateur Status at Any Age

The following are examples of acts at any age which violate the Definition of an Amateur Golfer and cause forfeiture of amateur status:

1. Professionalism

a. Receiving payment or compensation for serving as a professional golfer or identifying oneself as a professional golfer.

b. Taking any action for the purpose of becoming a professional golfer.

Note: *Such actions include applying for a professional's position; filing application to a school or competition conducted to qualify persons to play as professionals in tournaments; entering into an agreement, written or oral, with a sponsor or professional agent; agreement to accept payment or compensation for allowing one's name or likeness as a skilled golfer to be used for any commercial purpose; and holding or retaining membership in any organization of professional golfers.*

2. Playing for Prize Money

Playing for prize money or its equivalent in a match, tournament or exhibition.

Note: *A player may participate in an event in which prize money or its equivalent is offered, provided that prior to participation he irrevocably waives his right to accept prize money in that event. (See USGA Policy on Gambling for definition of prize money.)*

3. Instruction

Receiving payment or compensation for giving instruction in playing golf, either orally, in writing, by pictures or by other demonstrations, to either individuals or groups.

Exception: Golf instruction may be given by an employee of an educational institution or system to students of the institution or system and by camp counselors to those in their charge, provided that the total time devoted to golf instruction during a year comprises less than 50 percent of the time spent during the year in the performance of all duties as such employee or counselor.

4. Prizes and Testimonials

Acceptance of a prize or testimonial of the following character (this applies to total prizes received for any event or series of events in any one tournament or exhibition, including hole-in-one or other events in which golf skill is a factor):

(i) Of retail value exceeding $350; or

(ii) Of a nature which is the equivalent of money or makes it readily convertible into money.

EXCEPTIONS:

1. Prizes of only symbolic value (such as metal trophies).

2 More than one testimonial award may be accepted from different donors even though their total retail value exceeds $350, provided they are not presented so as to evade the $350 value limit for a single award. (Testimonial awards relate to notable performances or contributions to golf, as distinguished from tournament prizes.)

5. Lending Name or Likeness

Because of golf skill or golf reputation, receiving or contracting to receive payment, compensation or personal benefit, directly or indirectly, for allowing one's name or likeness as a golfer to be used in any way for the advertisement or sale of anything, whether or not used in or appertaining to golf, except as a golf author or broadcaster as permitted by Rule 1-7.

Note: *An advertisement may contain a player's name or likeness when it is customary to the business of such a player and contains no reference to the game of golf.*

6. Personal Appearance

Because of golf skill or reputation, receiving payment or compensation, directly or indirectly, for a personal appearance, except that reasonable expenses actually incurred may be received if no golf competition or exhibition is involved.

7. Broadcasting and Writing

Because of golf skill or golf reputation, receiving payment or compensation, directly or indirectly, for broadcasting concerning golf, a golf event or golf events, writing golf articles or books, or allowing one's name to be advertised or published as the author of golf articles or books of which he is not actually the author.

Exceptions:

1. Broadcasting or writing as part of one's primary occupation or career, provided instruction in playing golf is not included (Rule 1-3).

2. Part-time broadcasting or writing, provided (a) the player is actually the author of the commentary, articles or books, (b) instruction in playing golf is not included and (c) the payment or compensation does not have the purpose or effect, directly or indirectly, of financing participation in a golf competition or golf competitions.

8. Golf Equipment
Because of golf skill or reputation, accepting golf balls, clubs, golf merchandise, golf clothing or golf shoes, directly or indirectly, from anyone manufacturing such merchandise without payment of current market price.

9. Membership and Privileges
Because of golf skill or golf reputation, accepting membership or privileges in a club or at a golf course without full payment for the class of membership or privileges involved unless such membership or privileges have been awarded (1) as purely and deservedly honorary, (2) in recognition of an outstanding performance or contribution to golf and (3) without a time limit.

0. Expenses
Accepting expenses, in money or otherwise, from any source other than one on whom the player is normally or legally dependent to engage in a golf competition or exhibition.

Exceptions: A player may receive a reasonable amount of expenses as follows:
1. JUNIOR COMPETITIONS
   As a player in a golf competition or exhibition limited exclusively to players who have not reached their 18th birthday.
2. INTERNATIONAL TEAMS
   As a representative of a recognized golf association in an international team match between or among golf associations when such expenses are paid by one or more of the golf associations involved or, subject to the approval of the USGA, as a representative in an international team match conducted by some other athletic organization.
3. USGA PUBLIC LINKS CHAMPIONSHIPS
   As a qualified contestant in the USGA Amateur Public Links Championships proper, but only within limits fixed by the USGA.
4. SCHOOL, COLLEGE, MILITARY TEAMS
   As a representative of a recognized educational institution or of a military service in (1) team events or (2) other events which are limited to representatives of recognized educational institutions or of military services, respectively. In each case, expenses may be accepted from only an educational or military authority.
5. INDUSTRIAL OR BUSINESS TEAMS
   As a representative of an industrial or business golf team in industrial or business golf team competitions, respectively, but only within limits fixed by the USGA. (A statement of such limits may be obtained on request from the USGA.)
6. INVITATION EVENTS
   As a player invited for reasons unrelated to golf skill, e.g., a celebrity, a business associate or customer, a guest in a club-sponsored competition, etc., to take part in a golfing event.

Note 1: *A player is not considered to be "normally or legally dependent" upon an employer, a partner or other vocational source, and acceptance of expenses therefrom is not permissible.*

Note 2: Business Expenses—*It is permissible to play in a golf competition while on a business trip with expenses paid provided that the golf part of the expenses is borne personally and is not charged to business. Further, the business involved must be actual and substantial, and not merely a subterfuge for legitimizing expenses when the primary purpose is golf competition.*

Note 3: Private Transport—*Acceptance of private transport furnished or arranged for by a tournament sponsor, directly or indirectly, as an inducement for a player to engage in a golf competition or exhibition shall be considered accepting expenses under Rule 1-10.*

11. Scholarships
Because of golf skill or golf reputation, accepting the benefits of a scholarship or grant-in-aid other than in accord with the regulations of the National Collegiate Athletic Association or the Association of Intercollegiate Athletics for Women.

12. Conduct Detrimental to Golf
Any conduct, including activities in connection with golf gambling, which is considered detrimental to the best interests of the game.

Rule 2
Advisory Opinions, Enforcement and Reinstatement

1. Advisory Opinions
Any person who considers that any action he is proposing to take might endanger his amateur status may submit particulars to the staff of the United States Golf Association for advice. If dissatisfied with the staff's advice, he may request that the matter be referred to the Amateur Status and Conduct Committee for decision. If dissatisfied with the Amateur Status and Conduct Committee's decision, he may, by written notice to the staff within 30 days after being notified of the decision, appeal to the Executive Committee, in which case he shall be given reasonable notice of the next meeting of the Executive Committee at which the matter may be heard and shall be entitled to present his case in person or in writing. The decision of the Executive Committee shall be final.

2. Enforcement
Whenever information of a possible violation of the Definition of an Amateur Golfer by a player claiming to be an amateur shall come to the attention of the United States Golf Association, the staff shall notify the player of the possible violation, invite the player to submit such information as the player deems relevant and make such other investigation as seems appropriate under the circumstances. The staff shall submit to the Amateur Status and Conduct Committee all information provided by the player, their findings and their recommendation, and the Amateur Status and Conduct Committee shall decide whether a violation has occurred. If dissatisfied with the Amateur Status and Conduct Committee's decision, the player may, by written notice to the staff within 30 days after being notified of the decision, appeal to the Executive Committee, in which case the player shall be given reasonable notice of the next meeting of the Executive Committee at which the matter may be heard and shall be entitled to present his case in person or in writing. The decision of the Executive Committee shall be final.

Upon a final decision of the Amateur Status and Conduct Committee or the Executive Committee that a player has violated the Definition of an Amateur Golfer, such Committee may require the player to refrain or desist from specified actions as a condition of retaining his amateur status or declare the amateur status of the player forfeited. Such Committee shall notify the player, if possible, and may notify any interested golf association of any action taken under this paragraph.

3. Reinstatement
The Executive Committee shall have sole power to reinstate a player to amateur status or to deny reinstatement.

Each application for reinstatement shall be decided on its merits.

In considering an application for reinstatement, the Executive Committee shall normally be guided by the following principles:
a. PROBATION

The professional holds an advantage over the amateur by reason of having devoted himself to the game as his profession; other persons violating the Rules of Amateur Status also obtain advantages not available to the amateur. They do not necessarily lose such advantage merely by deciding to cease violating the Rules.

Therefore, an applicant for reinstatement to amateur status shall undergo probation as prescribed by the Executive Committee.

Probation shall start from the date of the player's last violation of the Definition of an Amateur Golfer unless the Executive Committee decides that it shall start from the date when the player's last violation became known to the Executive Committee.

b. PROBATIONARY PERIOD

A probationary period of two years will normally be required. The Executive Committee, however, reserves the right to *extend* or *shorten* such period. Longer periods will normally be required of applicants who have played extensively for prize money; shorter periods will often be permitted in the cases of applicants who were in violation of the Rules one year or less.

Players of national prominence who have been in violation for more than five years shall not normally be eligible for reinstatement.

c. ONE REINSTATEMENT

A player shall not normally be reinstated more than once.

d. STATUS DURING PROBATION

During probation an applicant for reinstatement shall conform with the Definition of an Amateur Golfer.

He shall not be eligible to enter competitions limited to amateurs except that he may enter competitions solely among members of a club of which he is a member, subject to the approval of the club. He may also, without prejudicing his application, enter, as an applicant for reinstatement, competitions which are not limited to amateurs but shall not accept any prize reserved for an amateur.

e. FORM OF APPLICATION

Each application for reinstatement shall be prepared, in duplicate, on forms provided by the USGA.

The application must be filed through a recognized amateur golf association in whose district the applicant resides. The association's recommendation, if any, will be considered. If the applicant is unknown to the association, this should be noted and the application forwarded to the USGA, without prejudice.

USGA Policy on Gambling

The Definition of an Amateur Golfer provides that an amateur golfer is one who plays the game as a non-remunerative or non-profit-making sport. When gambling motives are introduced, problems can arise which threaten the integrity of the game.

The USGA does not object to participation in wagering among individual golfers or teams of golfers when participation in the wagering is limited to the players, the players may only wager on themselves or their teams, the sole source of all money won by players is advanced by the players and the primary purpose is the playing of the game for enjoyment.

The distinction between playing for prize money and gambling is essential to the validity of the Rules of Amateur Status. The following constitute golf wagering and not playing for prize money:

1. Participation in wagering among individual golfers.
2. Participation in wagering among teams.

Organized amateur events open to the general golfing public and designed and promoted to create cash prizes are not approved by the USGA. Golfers participating in such events without irrevocably waiving their right to cash prizes are deemed by the USGA to be playing for prize money.

The USGA is opposed to and urges its Member Clubs, all golf associations and all other sponsors of golf competitions to prohibit types of gambling such as: (1) Calcuttas, (2) other auction pools, (3) pari-mutuels and (4) any other forms of gambling organized for general participation or permitting participants to bet on someone other than themselves or their teams.

The Association may deny amateur status, entry in USGA Championships and membership on USGA teams for international competitions to players whose activities in connection with golf gambling, whether organized or individual, are considered by the USGA to be contrary to the best interests of golf.

PRINCIPAL CHANGES SINCE 1979
Definitions

6. Ball Lost
Amended to provide that provisional ball becomes ball in play if played from point nearer hole than place where original ball likely to be, rather than a point beyond where original likely to be.

13. Ground Under Repair
Amended to provide that stakes and lines defining margins are in such ground, rather than not in such ground.

14. Hazards
Amended to provide that stakes and lines defining margins of water and lateral water hazards are in such ground, rather than not in such ground. Recommended colors for such stakes and lines specified.

Rules

9-2. Indicating Line of Play
Amended to permit a mark to indicate line of play provided mark is removed before stroke played.

10. Information as to Strokes Taken
Broadened to (1) cover giving of wrong information as to score in match play after play of hole completed and (2) provide that, in match play, a player is deemed to give wrong information if he has incurred a penalty and does not inform his opponent as soon as possible.

11-1. Claims and Penalties
Amended to provide for reopening of completed match or stroke play competition only if wrong information knowingly given.

11-5. Stroke Play; Doubt as to Procedure
Amended to make it more usable without risk of penalty in cases of doubt as to procedure and to permit a competitor to choose which ball he wants to score with if the Rules permit.

13-2. Playing Outside Teeing Ground; Stroke Play
Previously, competitor counted strokes played from outside teeing ground and then played from within teeing ground; now competitor incurs two-stroke penalty and plays from within teeing ground and strokes played from outside teeing ground do not count.

16. Ball Played as it Lies
Clause added giving free relief for ball embedded in own pitch-mark in closely mown area through the green.

21. Playing a Wrong Ball or from a Wrong Place
Text rearranged and clause added to permit competitor who plays from wrong place in stroke play to rectify serious breach of Rules.

22-2c. When to Re-Drop
Broadened to require re-drop if ball dropped from off putting green rolls onto green.

22-3a. How and Where to Place
Amended to permit ball to be placed only by the player or his partner, but a ball to be replaced may in addition be replaced by the person who lifted it.

23. Identifying or Cleaning Ball
Penalty for breach reduced to one stroke to make Rule consistent with Rule 27-1c.

24. Ball Interfering with Play
Amended along with Rules 35-2a and 35-3a so that all situations involving interference will be covered and relief for mental as well as physical interference will be provided.

26-2b. Ball in Motion Stopped or Deflected by Opponent
Penalty eliminated if ball accidentally stopped or deflected. Player has option to replay. Rules 40-2a and 40-3c covering such deflection in multi-ball play similarly amended.

28. Ball Unfit for Play
Amended to define unfit for play. Player now required to announce intention to proceed under this Rule to opponent or marker. Previously, player required to invoke Rule in the presence of the opponent or marker.

31-2b(i). Relief from Immovable Obstruction Through the Green
Amended to require player to drop ball within one club-length of nearest point of relief, rather than two club-lengths. Rules 32 and 35-lj similarly amended.

32. Casual Water, Ground Under Repair, etc.
Clause added to permit player to probe for lost ball and not incur penalty if ball moved.

35-1c. Damage to Putting Green
Broadened to permit player to repair an old hole plug as well as damage caused by the impact of a ball.

35-1k. Ball to be Marked when Lifted
Amended to make it consistent with Rule 27-1c re ball lifted purposely by player without authority.

37. The Player
Clause 6b amended to permit player who has discontinued play (in accordance with the Rules) during play of a hole to substitute another ball when play resumed.

Rules of Amateur Status

2-3b. Reinstatement; Probationary Period
Amended to provide that applicant for reinstatement in violation for one year or less often entitled to reduction in probationary period. Previously, Rule provided reduction usually not granted if such applicant played for prize money more than three times.